Limited Warfare in the Nuclear Age

Robert A. Doughty
United States Military Academy

Ira D. Gruber
Rice University

Roy K. Flint
United States Military Academy

Mark Grimsley
The Ohio State University

George C. Herring
University of Kentucky

Donald D. Horward
Florida State University

John A. Lynn
University of Illinois

Williamson Murray
The Ohio State University

D. C. Heath and Company

Lexington, Massachusetts   Toronto

Address editorial correspondence to:

D. C. Heath and Company
125 Spring Street
Lexington, MA 02173

Acquisitions: *James Miller*
Development: *Pat Wakeley*
Editorial Production: *Melissa Ray*
Design: *Alwyn R. Velásquez*
Photo Research: *Picture Research Consultants, Inc./Sandi Rygiel
& Pembroke Herbert*
Art Editing: *Diane Grossman*
Production Coordination: *Richard Tonachel*

The views expressed herein are those of the authors and do not purport to reflect the position of the United States Military Academy, the Department of the Army, or the Department of Defense.

International Standard Book Number: 0-669-41682-7

10 9 8 7 6 5 4 3 2 1

PREFACE

Limited Warfare in the Nuclear Age was first published as part of a larger history, *Warfare in the Western World*. We wrote that larger history to provide a coherent, readable, and authoritative account of the past four centuries of military operations in the West—to explain, as clearly as possible, how the waging of war has changed from one era to another since the beginning of the seventeenth century. Although we examined the underlying developments in population, agriculture, industry, technology, and politics that affected warfare, we focused on the employment of armed forces. We were most interested in operations, in the conduct of relatively large forces across a specific theater of war. Although we included warfare at sea and in the air as well as joint operations, we concentrated on fighting ashore. In short, we set out to write a sound and readable history of military operations in the West since 1600, a history that would appeal to students, general readers, and anyone seeking an authoritative reference on warfare.

Like its parent volumes, *Limited Warfare in the Nuclear Age* was designed to provide a coherent, readable, and authoritative history of military operations—specifically on the period since the creation of atomic and nuclear weapons. Robert Doughty wrote the chapter on the effect of atomic and nuclear weapons on warfare, Roy Flint that on the Korean War, and George Herring that on the Vietnam War. Doughty also wrote the chapters on the Middle Eastern wars and on warfare since the end of the Cold War.

As the authors explain, Cold War competition and tensions caused numerous armed conflicts after World War II, but the threat of atomic and nuclear weapons shaped the conduct of those wars and ensured that they remained limited. Because the existence of nuclear weapons created the possibility of a small crisis escalating into a vast nuclear exchange, the superpowers sought to deter their use. They nonetheless grappled with each other during the Cold War by every means short of direct combat or nuclear exchange. The Korean War was the first major conflict of the Cold War, and though it witnessed few innovations in warfare, Korea became a model for limited war in the newly born atomic era, demonstrating alternative ways of gaining national objectives without resorting to atomic war. The Vietnam War witnessed important innovations in warfare, particularly in technology, and brought home the complexities of waging limited war in the nuclear era. Numerous other wars—many of which had no links or only weak links to the Cold War—occurred in the post–World War II period, but those in the Middle East assumed a special significance because of that region's strategic importance and because of the advanced weapons and equipment used in the conflicts. Despite great loss of lives and immense destruction, the wars in Korea, Vietnam, and the Middle East remained limited.

When the Cold War ended in 1989–1990, the confrontation between the two superpowers and their allies faded away, but a more complicated world, split by national, religious, ethnic, and regional differences, emerged.

As violence and turmoil threatened to spread, national and international leaders often considered military intervention, relying on gains in strategic mobility developed during the Cold War. The first major conflict of this most recent period occurred when an international coalition of states responded to Iraqi aggression against Kuwait. As other conflicts appeared, the United Nations became involved more frequently in international peace-keeping and peace-enforcement operations. Doubts soon arose, however, about the ability of the United Nations to prevent local conflicts from escalating beyond the usual bounds of limited warfare into much larger and more destructive wars.

The authors of this volume have succeeded in locating warfare in the nuclear age in the broader history of warfare in the Western world. They, like the other authors of *Warfare in the Western World*, have benefitted from the writings and comments of many specialists and colleagues. We are all particularly indebted to Richard Kohn and John Shy, who read carefully an entire draft of the text and drew on their remarkable understanding of military history and sharp critical judgment to suggests ways of improving the whole. We are grateful to all who have had a part in creating *Warfare in the Western World* in general and *Limited Warfare in the Nuclear Age* in particular. We do not imagine that we will have satisfied all our critics; we do hope that they and other readers will continue to share their knowledge of warfare with us.

R. A. D. and I. D. G.

CONTENTS IN BRIEF

CONTENTS

MAP SYMBOLS

The symbols shown below are used on the maps in this volume. Most of the symbols suggest the organization of units in particular campaigns or battles. The reader should understand that the organization of military units has changed over time and has varied from army to army or even within armies. For example, the composition and size of Napoleon's corps varied within his own army and differed from those of his opponents; they also differed dramatically from those of armies later in the nineteenth century. The symbols thus indicate the organization of a unit at a particular time and do not indicate its precise composition or size.

Division	XX ⬓
Corps	XXX ⬓
Army	XXXX ⬓
Army Group	XXXXX ⬓
Cavalry Screen	● ● ●
Armor	⬓
Airborne	⬧
Fort	¤
Mine	o—o—o—o
Bridge	‿
Boundary between Units	—xxxxx—

LIST OF MAPS

1

THE COLD WAR AND THE NUCLEAR ERA: ADJUSTING WARFARE TO WEAPONS OF MASS DESTRUCTION

The Birth of the Atomic Arms Race

Placing Increased Reliance on the Bomb

Achieving Strategic Parity and Controlling Nuclear Weapons

The Cold War was a clash of interests and ideas that dominated international relations from 1945 until 1990. As antagonisms between the United States and the Soviet Union hardened in the late 1940s, a series of crises sharpened ideological differences and heightened tensions. With the Soviet Union leading communist states and the United States leading Western democratic states, the first crises occurred in Europe, but the establishment of the People's Republic of China in 1949, followed by the North Korean invasion of South Korea, intensified and expanded the Cold War. While the Soviet Union and other communist powers attempted to consolidate and expand their influence, the United States and its allies sought to "contain" communism. For more than four decades, the confrontation between the two camps yielded numerous conflicts, such as the ones in Korea and Vietnam, as well as those in the Middle East and Southwest Asia. Some of these conflicts were "campaigns" in the broader and more dangerous Cold War, and they occurred despite the threat of a small crisis escalating rapidly into a world war.

Through the decades of rivalry, the existence of atomic or nuclear weapons shaped the nature of the Cold War and influenced virtually every issue in international security. For a brief period the United States held a monopoly on the atomic bomb, but the Soviets exploded their first atomic device in August 1949. That explosion signaled the beginning of a remarkable arms race that would extend over the next four decades. From the mid-1950s to the early 1960s political and military leaders considered the effect of the new weapons and resigned themselves to the use of those weapons in an emergency. After the Cuban Missile Crisis in October 1962, the Soviet Union embarked on a massive program to modernize its nuclear arsenal. As the Soviets approached strategic parity with the Americans, both sides began accepting arms control limitations over their nuclear arsenals. Only the eventual disintegration of the Soviet Union ended the Cold War and reduced the danger of a nuclear holocaust.

Since the use of nuclear weapons created the possibility of an Armageddon, the superpowers sought to deter their use but nonetheless grappled with each other by every means short of direct combat or nuclear exchange. Each provided military and economic assistance to its allies, and each sought to gain influence in the newly emerging nations of Africa and Asia. Although direct armed conflict between the superpowers never took place, Moscow and Washington provided direct and indirect support to opposing sides in numerous conflicts around the world. Using the number of war-related deaths as the criterion for defining a major conflict, the Stockholm International Peace Institute identified more than 160 major conflicts between 1945 and 1990. Though many were regional or were civil wars with no apparent link to the Cold War, others created the possibility of escalation, superpower involvement, and the spilling over of war into Europe, where the vast forces of the North Atlantic Treaty Organization and the Warsaw Pact faced each other across the boundary of a divided Germany. Almost no one doubted that a conflict between these huge forces would escalate into a nuclear holocaust.

In the end, the introduction of atomic and nuclear weapons revolutionized the nature of strategy and imposed limitations on war to avoid the employment of these weapons. The value of nuclear weapons lay in their not being used and in their power to deter an opponent from using them or even using conventional weapons. Their introduction made the era of the Cold War unlike any other in the history of warfare.

The Birth of the Atomic Arms Race

Before the United States entered World War II, scientists had worked out the theoretical foundations of an atomic bomb. Fearful that Germany would develop and use an atomic bomb first, the physicist Leo Szilard convinced Albert Einstein to send a letter to President Franklin D. Roosevelt that explained the nature of atomic energy and how it could be fashioned into a weapon of unprecedented power. This letter led to the creation in 1942 of a highly secret program named the Manhattan Project, which became the largest, most expensive, and most secret program of World War II. Placed under the overall direction of the U.S. Army and led by Major General Leslie R. Groves, the army engineer who had just finished designing and building the Pentagon, and Dr. J. Robert Oppenheimer, a brilliant theoretical physicist, the project commanded the highest priorities for scarce wartime resources and involved many leading physicists, mathematicians, and chemists from the scientific community. Oppenheimer and his colleagues tested an atomic device for the first time in the desert of southern New Mexico on July 16, 1945.

After Germany surrendered in May 1945, some American scientists questioned whether the new weapon should be used against Japan; they believed Japan would fall inevitably to conventional forces. Political and military leaders believed, however, that using the bomb on Japan would shorten the war, save the lives of American soldiers, and perhaps influence the postwar expansionist behavior of the Soviets. The subsequent dropping

Major General Leslie R. Groves and Dr. J. Robert Oppenheimer in September 1945. The two hardly could have been less alike in appearance, personality, and politics.

of an atomic bomb on Hiroshima, Japan, on August 6, 1945, and another one on Nagasaki three days later brought the existence of the atomic bomb into the open and engendered much concern about its use. Though more people had died in some conventional bombing raids—Dresden, for example—the shock of Hiroshima and Nagasaki and the possibility of such weapons being employed in the future horrified the world.

The Americans Adapt to the Atomic Bomb

Following World War II, President Harry S Truman laid the groundwork for American atomic policy. From the beginning he regarded the atomic bomb as fundamentally different from other military arms. For a time he hoped that diplomatic initiatives at the United Nations (the Baruch Plan) would convince the Soviets to accept international control of atomic weapons, but deepening hostilities doomed the proposal. Concerned about the effects of atomic warfare, he reserved for himself the authority to order use of the bomb. Under the provisions of the Atomic Energy Act of 1946, Congress vested a completely civilian commission with control over the American atomic energy program. Scientific and technical knowledge about the atomic program, as well as production decisions, became hidden behind an unprecedented wall of secrecy. As a consequence, American war planners often worked in the early years of the atomic era without specific reference to the size, character, and capabilities of the American atomic arsenal. Recently declassified documents suggest that not even President Truman received a formal accounting until 1947 of how many weapons the United States actually possessed at any time.

As the Cold War intensified, the United States confronted the question of its role in the nuclear age. Americans watched uncomfortably as the Soviets refused to withdraw from Iran and then took over Czechoslovakia; they became even more concerned when Greek Communists attempted to overthrow Greece's government. Concluding that the United States had to take action against what seemed to be Soviet expansionist policies, Truman appeared before a joint session of Congress on March 12, 1947, and said, "I believe that it must be the policy of the United States to support free peoples who are resisting attempted subjugation by armed minorities or by outside pressures." In an attempt to revive Europe, the United States subsequently announced the Marshall Plan in June 1947. The core of the new policy of "containment" appeared in a famous article in *Foreign Affairs* in July 1947. The anonymous author, who was later identified as George F. Kennan, stated, "[T]he main element of any United States policy toward the Soviet Union must be that of a long-term, patient but firm and vigilant containment of Russian expansive tendencies." Kennan proposed opposing force with force and preventing the Soviets from expanding.

The atomic bomb provided partial answers to the question of how the United States could "contain" the USSR. In August 1947, strategic planners in the Joint Chiefs of Staff completed a war plan—code-named "Broiler"—which attempted to integrate atomic weapons into the American war machine. Recognizing that the bomb conferred a "tremendous strategic advantage" upon the United States and its allies, the planners of Broiler called for an "air-atomic campaign" very early in a war against Soviet targets that were chosen less for their military than their psychological importance. The campaign focused upon key governmental and other targets whose destruction would shock and unhinge the Soviet government. Though the target list in Broiler called for dropping thirty-four bombs on twenty-four cities, the United States had no fully assembled bombs and no capability to produce any quickly, and its more traditional means of military power had declined precipitously.

One of the first crises in which atomic weapons played a role—though an ambiguous one—occurred in the spring of 1948 when Truman responded to the Berlin Blockade. The Soviets had cut off all rail and road traffic to the western sections of Berlin, and he ordered an airlift of food and fuel supplies for the beleaguered people of the city. Part of his response included the deployment of sixty B-29s to airbases in Great Britain. Even though no atomic bombs actually left the United States, an administration spokesman pointedly announced that the aircraft were "nuclear capable." On May 12, 1949, the Soviets ended the blockade by once again permitting movement by land from West Germany into West Berlin and restoring gas and electric service. Flying more than 1.4 million metric tons of food, coal, and other supplies into Berlin apparently did more to end the blockade than deploying nuclear aircraft to Britain.

Toward the close of 1948 the United States had about one hundred atomic bombs in its stockpile, and its war plans emphasized a sudden atomic attack against the Soviet Union. Under the demanding leadership of General Curtis LeMay, the Strategic Air Command had developed the capability of delivering 80 percent of the American atomic stockpile in a single strike on the Soviet Union. One war plan—code-named "Fleetwood"—called for the delivery of 133 atomic bombs on seventy Soviet cities. Despite the emphasis on an "air-atomic campaign," the United States did not reject the possibility of a limited conventional campaign. It believed a future war would begin with a surprise attack by an enemy, to which the United States would respond with a massive atomic attack. As the aggressor reeled under an atomic attack, the United States would mobilize and employ its conventional forces. This view of future war permitted the United States the luxury of giving priority to strategic forces, while providing only minimum support to conventional forces. After all, planners argued, the employment of the bomb would provide the time necessary to prepare U.S. conventional forces.

An even greater emphasis on the atomic bomb, however, appeared in late 1949 in a new war plan code-named "Offtackle." Despite serious interservice differences, the 1950 budget reduced conventional capabilities even further. From the perspective of air-power advocates, atomic weapons seemed to need no assistance from armies except perhaps to occupy the smoking ruins of devastated cities. Air-power advocates also envisaged only limited roles for navies, including atomic bombs dropped from carrier aircraft. In what was later called the "Admirals' Revolt," the navy attempted to roll back the air-atomic emphasis, characterizing the new B-36 bombers as a "billion-dollar blunder." Nonetheless, American strategic forces flourished while conventional forces withered.

The Soviet Bomb, the Thermonuclear Bomb, and NSC-68

After failing to establish international control over atomic energy, the United States expected to maintain a monopoly over the bomb for some time and ruled out sharing scientific information with the USSR. General Groves confidently predicted it would take the Soviets ten to twenty years to produce a bomb. As early as 1939, however, Soviet scientists had started their own project to develop a bomb. By 1941, they had a cyclotron ready for experiments. The German invasion of the USSR stalled the Soviet atomic project until 1943, when the physicist Igor V. Kurchatov began directing a rejuvenated program. On August 29, 1949, in Central Asia, the Soviet Union exploded its first atomic device. The shock of America's losing its monopoly over atomic weapons was magnified by the fall of Nationalist China to the Chinese Communists in late 1949.

In response to these events, Truman formally authorized in January 1950 the building of the thermonuclear, or hydrogen, bomb—even though the Soviet Union would not have atomic weapons in large numbers or the capability to deliver them against the United States for several years. He also directed the formation of an ad hoc group of officials from the state and defense departments to conduct a review of American national security policies. This group would ultimately produce a memorandum designated NSC-68, which was to become one of the most important policy documents of the Cold War.

Presided over by Paul Nitze of the State Department's Policy Planning Staff, the ad hoc group's final report emphasized the expansionist nature of the Soviet Union and the danger such a power posed when armed with atomic weapons. Assuming the Soviets would eventually achieve atomic parity with the United States, the group considered prospects for defending Western Europe bleak. If the United States could not count on atomic weapons as its ultimate card, then conventional forces had to be ready to bear added burdens. The only recourse, Nitze's group believed, was to improve atomic and conventional forces simultaneously. The report also emphasized the adequacy "for the moment" of the American atomic retaliatory capability, but in the event of a "surprise blow," the United States had to be capable of surviving this attack and mounting an immediate counterattack. The authors of NSC-68 argued for the rejuvenation of the defense establishment so its ready combat power could deter the Soviets from a direct confrontation. With the Soviets' continuing to improve their atomic capabilities, the report signaled the eventual emergence of deterrence as a prime feature of American policy. The Americans would soon conclude that the value of their atomic weapons lay less in their actual use than in the threat of their use and that fear of retaliation would constrain an enemy from using them or creating a crisis in which they might be used.

Even though President Truman and the National Security Council formally approved NSC-68 in April 1950, chances were remote that this ambitious and expensive program would ever come to fruition. The United States still had vast superiority in atomic weapons over the Soviet Union, at least for a time, and possession of the bomb still worked as a powerful incentive for those who sought to limit government spending. To these critics, the time required for the Soviets to gain the capability to inflict significant damage on the United States seemed too long to warrant the kind of expensive defense buildup recommended by NSC-68. Truman himself was not entirely convinced of the need for rearmament.

And there the matter would have rested but for the attack, barely two months later, upon South Korea by the North Korean army on June 24, 1950. The limitations of the bomb were about to be made manifest.

The Korean War and the Truman Rearmament

Following the North Korean attack, many American political and military leaders feared that Moscow had directed the invasion as a diversionary move in preparation for a Soviet advance against Western Europe. Aware of the limitations of American power, the Joint Chiefs recommended the prompt abandonment of South Korea if the Soviets moved against Europe. Additional questions about Soviet motivations appeared in November 1950 when the Chinese Communists intervened in the war.

As a hedge against the much-feared invasion of Western Europe, Truman deployed atomic weapons to forward positions in Great Britain and the Mediterranean; however, he sent none to the western Pacific. The Joint Chiefs of Staff decided that the Korean peninsula was unsuitable for the use of atomic weapons. They believed Korea had no worthy targets, no industrial complexes or centers of military power that would warrant the use of any atomic weapon then in the arsenal. Additionally, they believed the rugged Korean terrain would limit the full effect of any atomic weapon, even against such targets as large troop concentrations. General Omar Bradley considered the idea of using these weapons in this conflict as "preposterous."

At a news conference in November 1950, President Truman nevertheless hinted broadly that atomic weapons might in fact be used in Korea. The North Koreans gave no sign they had heard, or taken seriously, the president's veiled threat, but Truman's comment alarmed the public in both the United States and Europe. British Prime Minister Clement R. Attlee immediately flew to Washington for talks with Truman, who reassured him that he would not really use the bomb. Like General Bradley and most of his other military advisors, the president feared that the real war lay elsewhere in the uncertain future and that America's atomic advantage would only be wasted on the Chinese. The Korean War thus remained limited, but it served as a catalyst for the implementation of the provisions of NSC-68, including a massive rejuvenation of the American armed forces.

The Truman administration realized that atomic weapons did not provide answers to every national security question. In fact, the brief atomic monopoly had given the United States a false sense of security and power and failed to avert military confrontation. Nor had possession of atomic weapons changed operational or tactical methods, as proven by the fighting on the Korean peninsula, which differed little from that of earlier wars.

Placing Increased Reliance on the Bomb

When Truman left office in 1953, he left nearly 1,000 atomic weapons to his successor, Dwight D. Eisenhower. Though Truman never overcame his awe of the atomic or nuclear bomb, his successor would demonstrate no such discomfort (at least in public). Nuclear weapons were about to become the centerpiece of the new administration's foreign and military policies. In the process, nuclear power would take on a much more pervasive character than what would have been believed possible in the early days of the Cold War.

During the presidential campaign of 1952, Eisenhower had campaigned on promises to end the war in Korea and to reduce the federal budget significantly. When he took office, military costs accounted for 70 percent of federal spending. Eisenhower did not think American foreign and defense policy took advantage of nuclear weapons and disagreed with the Truman administration's attempts to balance nuclear and conventional arms; reducing conventional forces would pay the bill for Eisenhower's campaign promises. By placing greater reliance on nuclear arms, Eisenhower believed the risk of reducing American conventional combat power could be minimized.

Throughout 1953, the Eisenhower administration worked to establish a "New Look" in national security policy. Hints about a new strategy suggested a stronger reliance on strategic nuclear power and less reliance on traditional ground and naval forces. In October 1953, the chiefs of the military services received a National Security document called NSC 162/2, which provided clear guidance from the Eisenhower administration. NSC 162/2 stated: "In the event of hostilities, the United States will consider nuclear weapons to be as available for use as other munitions." In an address before the United Nations, Eisenhower, reflecting his recent approval of NSC 162/2, observed that "atomic weapons have virtually achieved conventional status within our armed forces." Additional information came from Secretary of State John Foster Dulles in January 1954 when he called for "massive retaliation" in response to Soviet aggression.

"Massive Retaliation" became a shorthand description of the new strategy. It did not mean, however, that the United States would automatically respond to Soviet aggression with a massive nuclear strike; instead, it meant the Americans might reply in kind or raise the stakes by employing nuclear weapons. In other words, an American response was certain, but its nature was not. Critics of the strategy, however, perceived it as an "all-or-nothing" strategy, particularly when public comments by Dulles hinted that an aggressor had to remain uncertain about how close to the "brink" the United States would go.

Limited Nuclear War

When the Eisenhower administration adopted NSC 162/2 in 1953, the concept of "limited nuclear war" emerged as an alternative short of general nuclear war. The first concepts for limited nuclear warfare had appeared in the years immediately after World War II. One of the key figures in the development of the atomic bomb, J. Robert Oppenheimer, for example, stated in the late 1940s that existing bombs were "too big" for the "best military use." As technical advances permitted the development of smaller and more rugged nuclear devices, interest in the United States in tactical nuclear weapons accelerated. Faced with the Soviets' having significant advantages in conventional forces, analysts argued that an army equipped with tactical nuclear weapons could defend successfully against an enemy many times its

The firing of the first atomic artillery shell from a 280-mm artillery gun. Such tests demonstrated the availability of nuclear weapons and the possibility of their being employed throughout a battle area.

own size and that such weapons could enable Western military forces to halt communist aggression. Robert E. Osgood, in his influential book *Limited War*, explicitly linked tactical nuclear weapons and limited war. He wrote, "Tactical nuclear weapons, especially the low-yield battlefield weapons, can play a decisive role in supporting containment by giving the United States an adequate capacity for limited war at a tolerable cost."

Technological advances quickly provided tactical nuclear weapons. In May 1953, a U.S. Army 280-mm gun became the first artillery piece to fire a nuclear round successfully. Shortly thereafter, the army deployed half a dozen of the huge guns to Europe, even though they had a range of only seventeen miles and weighed eighty-three tons. It also equipped some of its units with Honest John rockets, which had a range of about twenty-two miles. Recognizing the need for smaller and more mobile nuclear delivery means, the army eventually introduced nuclear rounds for artillery pieces as small as 155-mm and introduced a nuclear-capable, short-range rocket, the Davy Crockett, into maneuver battalions. The Davy Crockett had a yield of .02 kilotons and a range of 650–4,400 yards.

As the army added tactical nuclear weapons to its inventory, it also reconfigured its infantry divisions by creating "Pentomic Divisions," which contained five "battle groups" (actually reinforced battalions). The new design eliminated the brigade echelon and added tactical mobility and other assets in an attempt to construct an organization that could disperse and concentrate rapidly. Theorists believed the division could survive and fight on the nuclear battlefield by spreading its forces in a "checker board," rather than linear fashion. Relying on new equipment, much of which never became available, the Pentomic Division proved to be difficult to command and not at all mobile, and its existence turned out to be mercifully brief.

Increases in the number of tactical nuclear weapons, nonetheless, created great concerns about escalation, particularly as Soviet capabilities increased. American critics argued that any tactical nuclear exchange would invariably lead to an all-out nuclear exchange. And Europeans feared the possibility of numerous tactical nuclear explosions on their crowded continent. More important, the Soviet Union paid little attention to tactical nuclear considerations, believing any use of nuclear weapons would initiate general nuclear war. In a key speech before the Supreme Soviet of the USSR in January 1960, the Soviet minister of defense ruled out "limited nuclear warfare" and "tactical use of nuclear weapons." Despite the obvious danger of escalation, tactical nuclear weapons remained an important part of the American arsenal.

Technological Advances

Eisenhower's two terms as president included not only a revolution in strategy but also a revolution in the technology of nuclear weapons and in the means of delivering them. Since the beginning of the nuclear era, air force bombers in Strategic Air Command had played the most important role in plans for delivering nuclear weapons. When Eisenhower took office, the United States had a mixed fleet of one thousand strategic and not-so-strategic bombers, and he lost no time in approving development of a truly strategic manned bomber, the all-jet B-52 Stratofortress, due to reach operational status by 1955. About 500 of these intercontinental bombers supplemented the more limited B-47 Stratojets, and by 1959 the United States had approximately 1,850 bombers.

As the United States improved its bombers, it also developed smaller, more powerful nuclear devices whose effect would be measured in megatons, rather than kilotons. In 1951, on the small Pacific island of Eniwetok, the United States detonated two small fusion devices, and the following year it detonated at Eniwetok a thermonuclear device with a force equal to 10 million tons of TNT, which was vastly larger than the bomb dropped on Hiroshima (equivalent to 14,000 tons of TNT) and the one dropped on Nagasaki (equivalent to 20,000 tons of TNT). The Soviet Union tested its own nuclear device in 1953. The United States tested an air-deliverable nuclear bomb in March 1954 but did not drop one from an airplane until May 1956. By the late 1950s, a B-52 bomber could deliver four nuclear bombs.

As technological improvements made nuclear weapons much smaller and also much more powerful, the missile began to challenge the manned bomber as the best means of delivery. By the mid-1950s, the air force was at work on two different Intercontinental Ballistic Missiles (ICBMs), the Titan and the Atlas, meant to deliver a one-megaton warhead at ranges of 5,500 and 6,250 miles, respectively. The first Atlas ICBMs became operational in the United States in 1959. The army entered the age of nuclear missiles in earnest with its own intermediate-range missiles. The Corporal became operational in 1953 with a 75-mile range, the Redstone in 1956 with a 225-mile range, and the Jupiter in 1957 with a range of 1,500 miles. Such missiles could reach far beyond the traditional area of concern of even the most senior ground commanders, leading to an intense debate between the army and air force about areas of responsibility.

The navy took a different atomic tack, investing initially in atomic propulsion for its fleet, especially its submarines. As early as 1951, however, it deployed nuclear-capable aircraft on its carriers, and three years later all carriers bore nuclear weapons and the aircraft to deliver them. Though the navy did not commission the world's first nuclear-powered aircraft carrier, the USS *Enterprise*, until November 1961, it commissioned the world's first nuclear-powered submarine, the USS *Nautilus*, in September 1954. At the end of the decade, the navy's Submarine-Launched Ballistic Missile (SLBM) program became feasible for submarines after smaller warheads and solid propellants became available. Initial plans called for the first missile-carrying submarine to be available in 1963, but increased concerns about the Soviet Union resulted in the first Polaris submarine, the USS *George Washington*, successfully launching its first missile while submerged in July 1960. Later versions of the missile increased its firing range from 1,375, to 1,700, to 2,850 miles. The age of the submarine-launched ballistic missile clearly had arrived.

The emergence of a Soviet nuclear threat made the gathering of intelligence particularly important. The United States created the National

Admiral H. V. Rickover directed construction of the USS *Nautilus*, the first nuclear-powered submarine. Its capability for sustained underwater operations was constrained only by the human limitations of its crew.

Security Agency in 1952; its mission was to conduct electronic eavesdropping on Russian communications systems. The new agency established radar stations in friendly countries along the Soviet perimeter and skirted Soviet borders with reconnaissance aircraft. As traditional sources of information—spies and refugees—began to dry up, the intelligence services resorted more and more to advanced technology to retrieve information. In 1956, the U-2, as the plane was called, became operational; it was capable of cruising above 70,000 feet, well beyond the ranges of Soviet air defenses. During the next four years, U-2s made dozens of spy flights over the Soviet Union before one was shot down by a new air-defense missile. By one informed estimate, the U-2 gleaned more than 90 percent of the West's strategic intelligence on the Soviet missile program before the flights ended. In time, satellites became the prime source of intelligence for both sides.

Meanwhile, like the Americans, the Soviets initially emphasized the long-range bomber. Their first important bomber was the Tu-16 Badger, which was similar to the American B-47 in performance. Entering into service in 1954–1955, it had the range to reach some cities in the United States on one-way flights from northern Siberia. In 1955, the Soviets introduced the Tu-20 Bear, which had a greater range and payload than the Badger, but not the American B-52. Although the Soviets had only a few hundred Bears and Badgers in service at the end of the 1950s, an intense debate erupted in the United States about the existence of a "bomber gap." A bomber gap did exist, but it was in favor of the Americans, not the Russians.

Motivated by inflated fears of Soviet bombers, the United States expended considerable effort and resources to defend itself against bombers with its Distant Early Warning line, numerous aerial interceptor squadrons, and land-to-air missiles that were nuclear armed.

As the United States prepared to defend itself against bombers, the Soviets made significant progress in the development of missiles. In August 1957 a Soviet SS-6 Sapwood ICBM traveled several thousand miles from its launch pad to its target in Siberia. Two months later, on October 4, 1957, an SS-6 rocket threw a 184-pound satellite called *Sputnik* into Earth orbit. One month later, the Soviets launched another satellite, weighing 1,121 pounds and carrying a live dog, into space. Though the Americans managed to launch a satellite, *Explorer I,* weighing thirty-one pounds, on January 31, 1958, they did not test the Atlas ICBM over its entire range for another year. Almost immediately, the "missile gap" replaced the bomber gap as Americans concluded that Soviet successes in space signaled their superiority in missile technology and numbers. Eisenhower, however, refused to panic. The U-2s, whose operations were known only to a few of the highest officials, had provided him with enough intelligence to know that the Soviets remained considerably behind the United States in strategic nuclear forces.

While Americans debated the implications of *Sputnik,* the Soviets began making slow progress in submarine-launched ballistic missiles. Between 1954 and 1957, the Soviets fitted several submarines with SS-N-4 Sark missiles, which had to be fired from the surface, rather than from underwater. The missile carried a nuclear warhead and had a range initially of 350 and later of 750 miles. Between 1958 and 1962, the Soviets equipped about thirty Golf and Hotel submarines with the SS-N-4 Sark. Not until 1968 did the Soviet navy complete a more modern submarine (the Yankee-class submarine) which carried sixteen missiles capable of being launched underwater and having a range of about 1,500 miles. The requirement for surface launching—in addition to the significant antisubmarine capability of the U.S. Navy—made the earlier Soviet submarines only a limited strategic threat to the United States. Nonetheless the Soviets had acquired the capability by the mid-1950s to inflict considerable damage on the United States, and that capability continued to expand.

Throughout much of the 1950s and 1960s, as demonstrated by the delusions associated with the "bomber gap" and the "missile gap," a significant difference existed between actual Soviet capabilities and American perceptions of those capabilities. The continued growth of Soviet missiles, however, dispelled all American hopes of fending off a Soviet nuclear strike. When the Soviets relied solely on bombers, the Americans could have destroyed many of the bombers before they dropped their bombs, but they had little or no defense against missiles. Though the United States maintained an overwhelming superiority, nuclear planners in the late 1950s recognized that the United States could not escape substantial damage in the event of a nuclear exchange.

Even though the Soviets remained far behind the Americans, a revolution in military affairs—according to Soviet writings—occurred in the Soviet armed forces between 1953 and 1960. Writers often compared the extent of the change to that which accompanied the introduction of gunpowder. In January 1960, Nikita S. Khrushchev underlined the extent of the change in an address to the Supreme Soviet of the USSR. He emphasized the decisiveness of nuclear weapons and threatened that if attacked, the Soviets would "wipe the country or countries attacking us off the face of the earth." A subsequent speech by the minister of defense highlighted the formation of new Strategic Rocket Forces and described them as "unquestionably the main service of the armed forces." In essence, the Soviets shifted from a primary focus on continental land warfare to a focus on global nuclear warfare. Military leaders believed that the revolution in military affairs compelled complete revisions in strategy, tactics, and force structure. As part of these revisions, the Soviets modified their thinking about the conduct of ground operations in the nuclear age and emphasized dispersion, mobility, high operating tempos, and multiple attacks on broad axes.

Thus, like the Americans, the Soviets acknowledged the profound effects of nuclear weapons on warfare. Changes in policy—influenced by the reduced size and increased power of nuclear weapons, the improved capabilities of manned bombers, the enhancement of missile range and accuracy, and the introduction of submarine-launched ballistic missiles—had achieved a military revolution, even if the only atomic bombs employed in combat were the two dropped on Japan at the end of World War II. For the moment the United States retained a position of superiority in nuclear affairs, but improvements in Soviet nuclear capabilities through the 1960s would eventually compel the United States to reevaluate its strategy of Massive Retaliation and to choose a different strategic path.

The Rise of the Defense Intellectuals

From the beginning, but particularly in the 1950s, much of the most important thinking in the United States about nuclear warfare was done by civilian intellectuals who traditionally had made a contribution to military thought but had never dominated the development of doctrine and equipment. Arguing that nuclear warfare was unique and answered to its own particular logic, civilian specialists provided much of the intellectual framework for nuclear thinking. They struggled to fit nuclear weapons within the framework of foreign policy and military affairs.

In a book entitled, *The Absolute Weapon*, Bernard Brodie laid down the fundamental outlines of nuclear deterrence—that the costs of retaliation in kind were too high for nations to contemplate using atomic warfare as a traditional means of defending their foreign policy interests. Brodie and his associates concluded that the real value of the atomic bomb lay not in its actual employment in war, but in the *threat* of its employment. In a now-famous passage, Brodie crafted the fundamental concept guiding what came to be called deterrence theory: "Thus far the chief purpose of our military establishment has been to win wars. From now on its chief purpose must be to avert them. It can have almost no other useful purpose." Additional thoughts came from other individuals, including J. Robert Oppenheimer, the physicist who had led the Los Alamos team during the Manhattan Project. In an essay published in *Foreign Affairs*, he depicted the Russians and Americans as "two scorpions in a bottle, each capable of killing the other, but only at the risk of his own life."

From these and other studies, the defense intellectuals conceived a wholly new vocabulary for the nuclear age and deployed it against the unconvinced defense establishment with breathtaking skill. "Counterforce" became the shorthand term for attacks against military targets. "Countervalue" was the touchstone for intentionally punitive attacks against "soft" targets such as cities and other psychologically valuable sites. "Stability" came to mean not a comfortable superiority such as the United States had enjoyed during the early years of the atomic era, but a kind of equilibrium reached when both sides were equally confident of destroying the other. Many outsiders found it difficult to accept the cold, logical language of nuclear theorists, some finding it as arcane as medieval scholasticism.

Particularly in the 1950s, Brodie and his colleagues—Albert Wohlstetter, Herman Kahn, and others—produced some of the most intellectually sophisticated work of the nuclear age. With their academic backgrounds, general contempt for traditional military thought, and quasi-official standing, the civilian strategists had a remarkable influence over nuclear thinking—and by extension, thinking about defense in general—from the Korean through the Vietnam wars.

Early Efforts to Rattle the Nuclear Saber

As for the effect of nuclear weapons on foreign policy, Eisenhower took advantage of the diplomatic power of the bomb early in his term. Attempting to unstick deadlocked negotiations with the Chinese, Eisenhower issued a discrete, ambiguous warning through the government of India that he might use atomic weapons against Chinese cities to force the Korean War to a conclusion. To back up his warning, he deployed atomic weapons to Okinawa, which was well within bomber range of both Korea and China. Though the effect of Eisenhower's atomic threat remains unclear, the Chinese did relent; several months later, the Korean armistice was announced.

The first full-fledged test of Eisenhower's new policy occurred early in 1954, a few months after the conclusion of the Korean armistice. In Indochina, the French army was gradually losing ground to a Vietnamese communist insurgency. The situation reached a crisis point in April 1954, when the French garrison at Dien Bien Phu seemed more than likely to succumb to its communist besiegers. Despite concerns about the effect of a French defeat on NATO's cohesion, Eisenhower refused to send American troops to bolster the French army in Indochina. He also refused to permit the employment of tactical nuclear weapons, even though Dien Bien Phu eventually fell.

A more direct contest with the Chinese Communists occurred over two small islands, Quemoy and Matsu, a few miles offshore from the Chinese mainland. Nationalist Chinese troops under Jiang Jieshi (Chiang

Kai-shek) had occupied the islands when they had lost the civil war in 1949. By September 1954, the Chinese Communists had concentrated troops on the mainland opposite these islands and had begun bombarding the Nationalist garrisons with artillery. Although Eisenhower never intended to use atomic weapons to solve the Quemoy-Matsu crisis, he equivocated in public. At a press conference in March, 1955, Eisenhower was asked to respond to a broad hint made earlier by Secretary of State Dulles that America would use some "small atomic weapons" if necessary. Eisenhower replied that smaller weapons could be used in such a case, "just as you would use a bullet or anything else."

The public furor that erupted over Quemoy and Matsu, along with all the talk about atomic weapons by administration officials and members of Congress, may well have been enough to dissuade the Chinese from invading the islands and attempting to take Formosa. All along, however, Eisenhower seemed to have no intention of committing American power, chiefly because he understood that the Chinese had no means of crossing the Formosa Strait against the opposition of the U.S. Seventh Fleet. The Chinese gave up their bombardment of the islands by April 1955 and agreed to diplomatic talks a while later.

The emergence of the Soviet Union as a strategic nuclear power altered the strategic equation. During the Suez Crisis of 1956, Israeli forces pummeled Egyptian forces in the Sinai while Anglo-French expeditionary forces seized the northern end of the Suez Canal and moved south quickly. With Egypt facing decisive defeat, the United States pressured the Israelis, British, and French to withdraw. Khrushchev went a step farther, however, and hinted of Soviet nuclear weapons landing in Paris and London and of Soviet "volunteers" pouring into Egypt. As with other crises, the effect of the nuclear threat was uncertain, but it was clear that more than one power could now rattle the nuclear saber.

Achieving Strategic Parity and Controlling Nuclear Weapons

Throughout the 1950s the strategy of Massive Retaliation came under severe criticism. As Soviet advances reduced American advantages in strategic arms, it no longer seemed credible to attempt to deter limited aggression by possibly escalating to a massive nuclear response. Thus, the likelihood of nuclear weapons, according to the critics, being employed against Soviet aggression decreased, as did the chances of effectively resisting communist aggression. Among those objecting most strenuously to American emphasis on strategic nuclear forces was a succession of U.S. Army general officers, including two chiefs of staff, General Matthew B. Ridgway and General Maxwell D. Taylor. To them, limited conflicts—particularly those in which conventional forces played a key role—seemed the way of the future, and they argued that the United States had to build strategically mobile conventional forces capable of meeting threats to national interests wherever they might appear.

During his campaign for the presidency, John F. Kennedy committed himself to reversing Eisenhower's Massive Retaliation strategy and substituting in its place a new strategy of "Flexible Response." Shortly after entering office in January 1961, he stated, "Any potential aggressor contemplating an attack on any part of the free world with any kind of weapons, conventional or nuclear, must know that our response will be suitable, selective, swift, and effective." In essence the president resolved to create multiple options so an American response could be tailored to a Soviet challenge. The new strategy required a larger number and variety of conventional forces, eventually leading the army, for example, to abolish its Pentomic divisions and to focus on conventional warfare.

When commissioned in 1961, the USS *Enterprise* was the largest ship ever built. It displaced 85,600 tons, measured over 1,100 feet, and carried a crew of 4,600, including 2,400 air personnel. Its vast range and great speed enabled the United States to project force over the entire globe.

The adoption of Flexible Response did not reduce the importance of nuclear weapons. Robert S. McNamara, the new secretary of defense, began developing the nuclear dimension of Flexible Response and emphasized the requirement, if deterrence failed, for greater flexibility and discrimination in the selection of nuclear targets. In June 1962, he said that "principal military objectives in the event of nuclear war . . . should be the destruction of the enemy's military forces, not of his civilian population." By refraining from an attack against enemy cities and by holding a large, strategic nuclear force in reserve, McNamara sought with a counterforce strategy to provide an adversary "the strongest possible incentive" to avoid striking American cities and to agree quickly to ending a war.

The new counterforce strategy proved to be expensive, for it required "powerful and well-protected" American nuclear forces. Additionally, the targeting of Soviet forces required more accurate and reliable delivery systems than targeting larger and more easily hit cities. The Kennedy administration took office at a time when the last of the first-generation ICBMs became operational (Atlas E in 1960, Titan I in 1962, and the Atlas F in 1962). Despite the costs involved, McNamara accelerated the entry of more accurate second-generation missiles (Minuteman I and Titan II) into the American arsenal and began eliminating first-generation missiles. He also reduced the number of manned bombers, primarily by phasing out the older B-47s. Recognizing the advantages of submarine-launched ballistic missiles, McNamara accelerated the development of Polaris submarines. The SLBMs represented the "third leg" (along with land-based ICBMs and manned bombers) of what became known as the TRIAD. To avoid substantial damage from a retaliatory or second strike, an adversary would have to destroy each leg of the TRIAD in a first strike. With the Americans' possessing three separate strategic systems for delivering nuclear weapons, however, the possibility of multiple strikes against the same target—or "overkill"—appeared, so in 1962 McNamara approved the Single Integrated Operational Plan (SIOP), which had been developed during the Eisenhower administration. By incorporating controlled options into the SIOP, the United States could hold in reserve a large strategic nuclear force and could manipulate nuclear warfighting instead of simply pulling a single trigger. By the mid-1960s, the United States had about 1,000 ICBMs, 650 SLBMs, and 650 manned bombers.

The Cuban Missile Crisis

The closest brush with nuclear Armageddon came not in the Eisenhower administration but in the Kennedy administration when the new president found few options to his liking in the Cuban Missile Crisis. The crisis grew out of Khrushchev's decision in early 1962 to place nuclear missiles in Cuba. Russian advisors, aircraft, and air-defense weapons accompanied the missiles, and in August 1962, an American U-2 spotted suspicious construction sites. As the reconnaissance flights continued, intelligence analysts identified more and more sites.

Despite Soviet assurances that no offensive missiles had been deployed in Cuba, a U-2 flight returned on October 14, 1962, bearing photographs that definitively revealed launch sites being prepared in western Cuba for medium-range (1,000 miles) ballistic missiles as well as long-range (2,200 miles) missiles. If the Soviets finished the sites and placed nuclear weapons at them, they would have the capability of covering with nuclear weapons much of the continental United States. Believing he could not permit the weapons to remain in Cuba, President Kennedy ordered a naval "quarantine" on October 22, 1962, to prevent Cuba from receiving any more Soviet equipment. He also insisted that any nuclear weapon launched from Cuba would be considered to have been launched from the Soviet Union and placed U.S. nuclear forces on the highest level of alert ever ordered, DEFCON-2 (Defense Condition 2), including the maintenance of fifty-seven nuclear bombers on a twenty-four hour flying readiness schedule. Another quarter of a million American troops also were placed in higher states of readiness. Meanwhile, Soviet commanders in Cuba received permission to use nuclear weapons in the event of an American invasion.

As the crisis intensified, Khrushchev offered to withdraw the missiles from Cuba in exchange for the Americans' removing Jupiter missiles from Turkey, lifting the naval blockade, and promising not to invade Cuba. Kennedy eventually accepted the offer but did not make his own concession public. After some tense moments at the naval picket lines, when Soviet and American ships faced off, the crisis passed. By October 27, all parties had backed off gingerly from the nuclear brink.

Both superpowers emerged from the Cuban Missile Crisis with a revitalized fear of nuclear consequences. Though Secretary of State Dean Rusk believed the Americans and Soviets came away from the crisis "more cautious and more thoughtful," the Soviets concluded that the American advantage in nuclear weapons had forced them to yield, and they subsequently embarked on an ambitious program to modernize their nuclear arsenal. Shortly after the crisis, a senior Soviet official told his American counterpart, "You Americans will never be able to do this to us again." A new period in the nuclear era had begun.

Mutual Assured Destruction

Though the American modernization program in the 1960s was impressive, that of the Soviets was even more so. A succession of new ICBMs entered the Soviets' Strategic Rocket Forces in the late 1960s. The SS-11 became operational in 1966, the SS-9 in 1967, and the SS-13 in 1969. The SS-11 became the most extensively employed Soviet ICBM. At the same time, the Soviets began to place their strategic weapons in hardened underground silos. Moreover, the Soviet Union accelerated in the mid-1960s the construction of submarines capable of launching strategic missiles. By 1970 the Soviet Union had surpassed the United States in number of operational ICBMs, 1,299 to 1,054.

As the Russians acquired a greater capability to retaliate directly against American cities, the Americans began to question a purely counterforce strategy and to look for other options. In February 1965 Secretary McNamara announced that the United States would rely on "Assured Destruction" to deter a Soviet attack. In essence, this meant the Americans would respond to an enemy nuclear attack by inflicting unacceptable damage on the Soviets, that is, an attack upon civilian as well as military targets. McNamara believed the possibility of massive destruction of Soviet cities would deter the enemy from launching a first-strike attack.

After the Soviets acquired an assured second-strike capability, the Americans modified their strategy again. In September 1967, McNamara added the word "mutual" to "assured destruction," thereby creating the unfortunate acronym, MAD, which suggested to many the insanity of holding the populations of both countries hostage. Nevertheless, Mutual Assured Destruction signaled an acceptance by the United States of its own vulnerability and the emergence of what McNamara called a "stable balance of terror." According to some analysts, the Soviet Union achieved "strategic parity" or a "rough equilibrium" in the early 1970s.

The Proliferation of Nuclear Weapons

For nearly two decades, the history of the nuclear era played out chiefly in the United States and the Soviet Union, but other powers began acquiring atomic or nuclear capability. Several months before the Soviets tested their atomic bomb in 1949, the British announced they would build their own atomic weapons. In October 1952, they tested their first atomic bomb on a small island northwest of Australia.

France's explosion of a bomb in the Sahara Desert in February 1960 signaled major changes in the nuclear arena. In his memoirs, Charles de Gaulle stated that one of his objectives had been for France "to acquire a nuclear capacity such that nobody could attack us without risking frightful wounds." It quickly became clear that the "nobody" included the United States. In November 1968, the French army's chief of the general staff published an article in which he announced that French nuclear forces, the *force de frappe*, would be capable of covering all points of the compass. In essence, he declared the independence of French nuclear forces. Other powers also acquired nuclear capabilities. In 1957, the Soviet Union agreed to provide defense assistance to Communist China, including assistance in nuclear matters. The Soviets cooperated fully with Chinese specialists who exploded their first nuclear device in October 1964.

With the number of nuclear powers increasing, many political and military leaders became increasingly concerned about the dangerous proliferation of nuclear technology. In August 1967, the United States and the Soviet Union jointly submitted to the U.N. Disarmament Commission a treaty to halt the spread of nuclear weapons. When ratified, the Nuclear Nonproliferation Treaty bound the signatory states with nuclear weapons not to supply them to other nations and those without nuclear weapons not to manufacture them. Though the pact was hailed as an epochal event, states throughout the world continued to seek nuclear technology. Communist

China denounced the treaty as a "plot," and in May 1974, India exploded its first nuclear device. Despite the sincerest of efforts, the "nuclear genie" had escaped from the bottle.

Arms Control Comes of Age

For almost two decades after World War II, little or no progress occurred in arms control. During the years when the United States had obvious superiority over the Soviet Union, Moscow often called for general and complete disarmament, but neither Moscow nor Washington accepted any real limitations or controls. In 1946, Bernard M. Baruch presented to the United Nations an American proposal for international control over the development and use of atomic energy, but the proposal foundered when the Soviets objected to on-site inspections. In 1955, President Eisenhower, hoping to lessen the danger of surprise attack, suggested having "Open Skies" over the USSR and the United States by permitting each to conduct flights over the other. The Soviets, however, denounced the plan as an espionage plot. Following the Cuban Missile Crisis, the two sides swiftly approved the Limited Test Ban Treaty of 1963. With over one hundred signatories, the treaty prohibited the testing of nuclear devices in space, the atmosphere, and underwater but allowed underground testing. Additional progress occurred as the two superpowers approached strategic parity, most notably the 1967

As the range of Polaris missiles grew from 1,375 to 2,850 miles, nuclear submarines carrying the missiles became more difficult to locate since they could hide in vastly larger areas of the ocean.

Nonproliferation Treaty. Several years of subsequent talks, however, failed to produce a breakthrough on limiting nuclear arms. In these and other efforts at arms control, distrust between the superpowers and the technical difficulties of verifying numbers and controlling technological advances created insurmountable obstacles.

Throughout the arms control discussions, verification of the number of an opponent's warheads remained impractical but became even more problematic when the United States began deploying missiles with multiple warheads. In 1964 it introduced the Polaris A-3 missile, which carried a multiple reentry vehicle (MRV) payload. When fired, the MRV would separate into individual reentry vehicles, or "bomblets," and strike an area in "shotgun" fashion. In 1968 the United States tested a multiple independently targeted reentry vehicle (MIRV) with the Minuteman III, which was an intercontinental ballistic missile with a range of about 9,300 miles. More accurate than the bomblets in the MRV warheads, the bomblets in the MIRV warheads could be directed with surprising precision against individual targets. The warhead of the Minuteman III carried three reentry vehicles, or bomblets, each with an estimated yield of about 200 kilotons. In 1970 the United States fitted its submarines with the Poseidon C-3 missile, which had a MIRV capability. The Soviet Union soon matched the technological developments in American strategic weapons. Testing of the SS-9 with a MRV warhead began in late 1968, and the fielding of Soviet missiles with MIRVs began in 1974.

The implications for nuclear strategy and arms control were enormous. Analysts contended that a preemptive nuclear strike by ICBMs with multiple warheads could inflict significant damage to fixed missile silos. Some concluded that immobile, undefended, land-based ICBMs were obsolete. Also, the existence of multiple warheads on a single missile made the number of warheads almost impossible to verify. Using satellites, both sides could detect and count missile launchers, but they could not count warheads. Technological advances had changed the rules for the nuclear game.

Despite the problems posed by MIRVs and verification, both sides slowly came to recognize in the late 1960s the "advantages" of a strategic balance and dreaded the costs of another round of nuclear improvements. For the most part, subsequent discussions between the superpowers took little notice of the increasing spread of nuclear weapons to other countries. Nonetheless, the bilateral superpower negotiations for the Strategic Arms Limitation Treaty (SALT), which began in Helsinki in late 1969, were not concluded until nearly three years later. SALT I, as it came to be known, called only for a freeze on building more ICBMs by both sides and restricted the United States and the Soviet Union to two Antiballistic Missile (ABM) sites each. The treaty did not include a limit on numbers of warheads. Despite its modest achievements, SALT I was an important first step in arms control.

The next round of SALT discussions also proceeded slowly. Meanwhile the Soviets tested a new, more powerful family of ICBMs: SS-17, SS-18, and SS-19. All of them had MIRVs. In June 1979, Jimmy Carter and Leonid Brezhnev finally signed the SALT II agreements, which capped strategic delivery systems for each side at no more than 2,250, and established a specific ceiling of 1,320 missiles with MIRVs.

Despite the apparent progress, controversy plagued the arms control process. One sensitive issue was that of U.S. plans to field the enhanced radiation bomb, which was also known as the "neutron bomb." This new device produced much greater radiation than a traditional weapon and thus had a greater effect on personnel in armored vehicles, which were relatively resistant to blast effects. This made it a useful weapon against the huge Soviet armored forces. Critics argued, however, that the new device made nuclear war more likely by blurring the distinction between nuclear and conventional war. The introduction of the cruise missile also added complexity to the nuclear equation. The missile used forward-looking radar to guide itself along the nap of the Earth to its target. Though many analysts doubted its capacity to kill hard targets such as ICBMs deep within their silos, its existence blurred the distinction between strategic and theater-level nuclear delivery systems. A protocol attached to the SALT II agreement established temporary bans on the deployment of mobile ICBM launchers and on longer-range cruise missiles. After an intense debate in the U.S. Senate about whether SALT II should be ratified, the treaty fell victim to renewed American doubts about Soviet intentions following their invasion of Afghanistan in December 1979.

Continued Innovation in Nuclear Technology

In the 1960s and 1970s, key American officials concluded that assured destruction was not enough and that the United States needed a wider range of options. In 1973, James Schlesinger, secretary of defense under President Richard M. Nixon, stated, "[W]e ourselves find it difficult to believe that we would actually implement the threat of assured destruction in response to a limited attack on military targets that caused relatively few civilian casualties." He then called for "a series of measured responses to aggression which bear some relation to the provocation." In July 1980, President Carter signed Presidential Directive 59, which incorporated many of Schlesinger's ideas; the document called for a "countervailing" nuclear strategy in which the United States would arrange its future arsenal so that it could fight a nuclear war at "any level of intensity," from limited nuclear exchange, to a theater-level war, to all-out nuclear war. Improvements in command and control, delivery systems, and accuracy had enabled the Americans to develop the capability to use their nuclear weapons in limited nuclear options against Soviet nuclear forces, conventional forces, or other military targets, and perhaps to control escalation all the way from the most limited use through an all-out nuclear exchange. In essence, the new policy signaled a move away from countervalue toward counterforce in U.S. strategy; it relied on delivery means for nuclear weapons becoming more precise and controls becoming more flexible. Nevertheless its announcement brought on a storm of criticism from those who believed the new policy increased the likelihood of nuclear weapons being employed in the future.

When Ronald Reagan became president in 1981, he was convinced that the Soviet nuclear forces were superior to those of the U.S., and he soon took steps to strengthen the U.S. nuclear arsenal. While refusing to revive SALT II, Reagan accelerated the employment of Trident nuclear submarines and Trident II missiles (an undersea long-range missile system that was begun in the early 1970s) and stood solidly behind the decision to deploy Pershing II and Tomahawk cruise missiles in the defense of Europe. He also poured money into the MX missile. Although Carter had initiated most of the new programs, it was Reagan who pushed them. From the Soviet perspective, the new president seemed to be waging economic warfare.

Among the most dramatic steps taken by President Reagan was the Strategic Defense Initiative, which initially envisaged a strategic missile defense in space using directed energy or lasers. After the use of laser weapons proved infeasible, a concept for kinetic energy interceptors replaced the notion of using lasers. Whatever its methods, the announcement of SDI created an international uproar and popular dissent. Critics saw the SDI program as a dangerous change, for the prospect of the United States' having a shield against a nuclear attack seemed to increase the chances of the Soviets' attacking before the shield was completed or to encourage the Americans to launch a first strike after the shield was erected. Either scenario could result in a nuclear holocaust. As the Soviet Union began to desintegrate and the threat of a Soviet attack receded, questions about the utility and expense of SDI increased. When Iraq's effort to develop nuclear weapons became apparent in the Persian Gulf War, however, proponents of SDI pointed out that nuclear weapons were no longer the monopoly of the superpowers and that up to fifteen states could possess nuclear weapons in the near future. They believed SDI could provide valuable protection against an attack from one of these powers.

As the 1980s ended, Mikhail S. Gorbachev, the Soviet head of state, eagerly sought additional curbs on nuclear weapons. In December 1987, Gorbachev and Reagan agreed to destroy all U.S. and Soviet intermediate-range nuclear missiles (300–3,000 miles). In July 1991, Gorbachev and President George Bush signed the long-awaited Strategic Arms Reduction Treaty (START). In essence, START cut Soviet strategic nuclear warheads from 11,012 to 6,163 and American warheads from 12,646 to 8,556. Following the dissolution of the Soviet Union, President Bush and President Boris N. Yeltsin of Russia signed START II in January 1993. The treaty limited Russia to 3,000 warheads and the United States to 3,500. The treaty also banned all long-range land-based missiles with multiple warheads. Bush concluded, "Today, the Cold War is over."

The proliferation of nuclear arms around the world, however, ensured that concerns about nuclear weapons did not disappear with the ending of the Cold War. In an indication of the increasing complexity of the nuclear environment, three of the successor states to the Soviet Union—Ukraine, Kazakhstan, and Belarus—expressed reservations about the START agreements. As the United States confronted the new strategic environment, it refocused the SDI program from providing protection against a Soviet attack to providing protection from "limited ballistic missile strikes, whatever their source." The new strategy of Global Protection against Limited Strikes (GPALS) signaled how dramatically the international situation had changed.

☆　　☆　　☆　　☆

Through the second half of the twentieth century, nuclear weapons affected many decisions and actions relating to international security and had dramatic effects on strategy and force structure. After World War II, the United States had only a few atomic weapons, but it had a monopoly over them. In subsequent years as the Cold War heated up, and as the United States adopted a policy of containing the USSR and communism, atomic weapons played an increasingly larger role in American military thinking. When the

Observers watch the explosion of an atomic shell. In mid-1955, the U.S. Army positioned a task force three kilometers from an exploding 30-kiloton atomic device and had them advance to within 900 meters of ground zero. Such exercises supposedly demonstrated the ability of ground forces to operate on a nuclear battlefield.

Soviet Union exploded an atomic and then a nuclear device, the United States lost its monopoly over the enormously destructive weapons, and deterrence became particularly important. For the rest of the Cold War, containment and deterrence remained significant American goals.

Following the Korean War, Eisenhower emphasized a strategy of Massive Retaliation, and nuclear weapons assumed a position of primacy in American military thinking. As the Soviets improved their nuclear capabilities, the Americans moved toward a strategy of Flexible Response, which relied on more balanced conventional and nuclear forces. After the Cuban Missile Crisis, the Soviet Union accelerated the development of its nuclear capabilities, and the United States adopted Assured Destruction and then Mutual Assured Destruction as its new strategy. Recognizing it could no longer maintain overwhelming superiority, the United States prepared to respond to a Soviet attack by destroying much of Soviet society.

The United States maintained its nuclear superiority until the early 1970s when the Soviet Union gained strategic parity. With nuclear forces in rough equilibrium and new technological advances threatening to upset the delicate balance or require vast new resources, political leaders became more agreeable to nuclear arms limitations. Meanwhile, the long-term evolution of American nuclear policy formally entered a new phase with the adoption of a countervailing strategy in July 1980. Instead of relying on Mutual Assured Destruction, the Americans had developed the capability to use nuclear weapons in limited nuclear options and sought to avoid an all-out nuclear exchange. Finally, the dissolution of the Soviet Union and the proliferation of nuclear weapons created a new strategic environment; the United States began shifting from an emphasis on retaliation against nuclear attack to defense against nuclear attack.

Though numerous wars occurred between 1945 and 1990, the only two bombs used in combat were those dropped on Hiroshima and Nagasaki, and thus concepts for nuclear war remained largely theoretical. The United States and the Soviet Union expended vast resources to develop strategies and forces for nuclear war, but they also devoted considerable effort and resources to avoiding such a war and to preventing a small war from escalating into a larger war. The initiation of an era of limited war thus emerged as one of the most important effects of the introduction of nuclear weapons.

SUGGESTED READINGS

Armacost, Michael H. *The Politics of Weapon Innovation: The Thor-Jupiter Controversy* (New York: Columbia University Press, 1969).

Bacevich, A. J. *The Pentomic Era: The U.S. Army between Korea and Vietnam* (Washington, D.C.: National Defense University Press, 1986).

Brodie, Bernard, ed. *The Absolute Weapon: Atomic Power and World Order* (New York: Harcourt, Brace and Company, 1946).

Brodie, Bernard. *Strategy in the Missile Age* (Princeton, N.J.: Princeton University Press, 1959).

Bundy, McGeorge. *Danger and Survival: Choices About the Bomb in the First Fifty Years* (New York: Random House, 1988).

Freedman, Lawrence. *The Evolution of Nuclear Strategy* (New York: St. Martin's Press, 1981).

Gaddis, John L. *Strategies of Containment* (New York: Oxford University Press, 1982).

Herken, Gregg. *The Winning Weapon: The Atomic Bomb in the Cold War, 1945–1950* (New York: Vintage Books, 1982).

Holland, Lauren H., and Robert A. Hoover. *The MX Decision: A New Direction in Weapons Procurement Policy* (Boulder, Col.: Westview Press, 1985).

Kaplan, Fred M. *The Wizards of Armageddon* (New York: Simon and Schuster, 1983).

Kissinger, Henry. *Nuclear Weapons and Foreign Policy* (New York: Harper, 1957).

Mandelbaum, Michael. *The Nuclear Question: The United States and Nuclear Weapons, 1946–1976* (Cambridge: Cambridge University Press, 1979).

Midgley, John J., Jr. *Deadly Illusions: Army Policy for the Nuclear Battlefield* (Boulder, Col.: Westview Press, 1986).

Neufeld, Jacob. *Ballistic Missiles in the United States Air Force, 1945–1960* (Washington, D.C.: Government Printing Office, 1989).

Newhouse, John. *War and Peace in the Nuclear Age* (New York: Alfred A. Knopf, 1989).

Osgood, Robert E. *Limited War: The Challenge to American Strategy* (Chicago: University of Chicago Press, 1957).

Porro, Jeffrey, ed. *The Nuclear Age Reader* (New York: Alfred A. Knopf, 1989).

Prados, John. *The Soviet Estimate: U.S. Intelligence Analysis and Russian Military Strength* (New York: Dial Press, 1982).

Rhodes, Richard. *The Making of the Atomic Bomb* (New York: Simon and Schuster, 1986).

Rose, John P. *The Evolution of U.S. Army Nuclear Doctrine, 1945-1980* (Boulder, Col.: Westview Press, 1980).

Rosenberg, David A. "The Origins of Overkill: Nuclear Weapons and American Strategy, 1945–1960," *International Security*, vol. 7, no. 4 (Spring 1983), pp. 3–71.

_____. "American Atomic Strategy and the Atomic Bomb Decision," *Journal of American History*, vol. 66, no. 1 (June 1979), pp. 62–87.

Sherwin, Martin J. *A World Destroyed: Hiroshima and the Origins of the Arms Race* (New York: Vintage Books, 1987).

Stares, Paul B. *The Militarization of Space: U.S. Policy, 1945–1984* (Ithaca, N.Y.: Cornell University Press, 1985).

Talbott, Strobe. *Deadly Gambits: The Reagan Administration and the Stalemate in Nuclear Arms Control* (New York: Alfred A. Knopf, 1984).

_____. *Endgame: The Inside Story of SALT II* (New York: Harper & Row, 1979).

Werrell, Kenneth P. *The Evolution of the Cruise Missile* (Maxwell Air Force Base, Ala.: Air University Press, 1985).

Wohlstetter, Albert. "The Delicate Balance of Terror," *Foreign Affairs*, vol. 37, no. 2 (January 1959), pp. 211–34.

2

KOREA: LIMITING WAR
TO AVOID ARMAGEDDON

**Rushing to War: The High
Cost of Unpreparedness**

**Changing War Aims and
a Changing War**

**Ending the War:
Politics as War**

The Korean War was the first major conflict of the Cold War; it began on June 25, 1950, when North Korean ground forces invaded South Korea. Armed forces from the United States and other members of the United Nations came to the aid of the South Koreans, and a three-year war resulted. After fighting a war of maneuver up and down the Korean peninsula for about a year, the combatants settled into deeply entrenched positions, reminiscent of World War I. As negotiations for ending the war began and the war became a stalemate, bitter battles erupted over minor outposts for small negotiating advantages. The issue of exchanging prisoners of war became a major obstacle to final agreement, prolonging the war until an armistice stopped the fighting on July 27, 1953.

While the Korean War witnessed few innovations in warfare, it demonstrated methods for gaining national objectives in the newly born atomic era. For the United States, the war was a "limited" war. To avoid provoking retaliation from the Soviet Union, American political leaders limited the geographic areas in which military commanders could operate, the strength of their forces, and the weapons to be used against the enemy. Communist forces suffered huge losses in the fighting and sought to achieve, through prolonged armistice negotiations, what they could not gain on the battlefield. They sought an advantageous political outcome by manipulating public opinion in the United States and among its allies, as well as throughout the nonaligned nations of the world. Thus the Korean War was less about tactical evolution than about political goals, the strategy to achieve those goals, and the operations designed to make the strategy succeed.

Rushing to War: The High Cost
of Unpreparedness

After World War II, antagonism between the Soviet Union and the United States grew as the two former allies became increasingly distrustful and suspicious of the other's motives. The first notable confrontation occurred in 1946 when the Soviets briefly refused to withdraw from Iran. More acute problems occurred in Turkey and Greece. The Soviets pressured the Turks for control of the straits of the Bosporus and Dardanelles and the return of territory lost at the end of World War I. When Greek Communists attempted to overthrow Greece's government, the Americans became particularly concerned, and President Truman pledged support to "free peoples who are resisting attempted subjugation by armed minorities or by outside pressures." This pledge came to be known as the Truman Doctrine. In an attempt to revive Europe, the United States established the Marshall Plan in 1947 and provided the economic base on which democratic reforms could be made. But international tensions increased with the Berlin Blockade in the spring of 1948, the explosion of a Soviet atomic device in August 1949, and the communist takeover of China in December 1949. During this series of crises, the United States adopted the policy, defined by George F. Kennan, of "a long-term, patient but firm and vigilant containment of Russian expansive tendencies."

In January 1950 President Truman directed officials from the departments of state and defense to conduct a broad assessment of American military needs. The resulting document, known as NSC-68, was the first comprehensive statement of national security policy since the end of World War II. To meet the threat posed by rapidly expanding Soviet capabilities, NSC-68 advocated an immediate buildup of U.S. and allied military strength in hopes that the United States might induce a change in Soviet policy while avoiding all-out war. The document called for the United States to have the capacity to wage either general or limited war and clearly emphasized that atomic weapons by themselves were insufficient for American national security needs. War broke out in Korea, however, before military readiness could be improved significantly.

Rapid demobilization after World War II had greatly affected American armed forces, but of all the services, the U.S. Army was in the worst shape to fight a war. In total, there were ten army divisions and eleven separate brigades on active duty in the spring of 1950. Of those forces, four infantry divisions were in Japan and immediately available to General of the Army Douglas MacArthur, Commander-in-Chief, Far East, and thereby the theater commander. But these forces were far from being combat ready. Except for the 25th Infantry Division, all were below their authorized peacetime strength of 12,500 men. Within the regiments, the number of battalions had been reduced from three to two and the tank company eliminated. The divisions' artillery was scaled down, and there were shortages of antitank mines, high explosive antitank ammunition, and spare parts for weapons. The divisions also had serious training problems. Although individual soldiers were reasonably well trained, units were not. When Lieutenant General Walton H. Walker took command of Eighth Army in the summer of 1949, training for combat finally took priority over occupation duties, but the demands of occupying and administering Japan continued to take their toll on combat readiness.

Failing to recognize the likelihood of war in Korea also had an effect on readiness. When World War II ended, the Soviets and the Americans entered Korea to administer the surrender of Japanese forces. At that time the 38th Parallel had no significance other than dividing Korea in such a way as to give the United States ports at Inchon and Pusan to facilitate the repatriation of Japanese troops. As the possibility of Korean unification became more remote, the South Koreans held elections in May 1948, and after the U.N. General Assembly recognized the newly elected government of Syngman Rhee in South Korea, the Soviets created and recognized the Democratic People's Republic of Korea. The 38th Parallel divided the two Korean states.

Throughout this period, the United States remained primarily concerned with unfolding events in Europe and demonstrated little interest in becoming deeply involved in Korea. By 1950, Kim Il Sung had risen to the top of the communist forces in North Korea and had assembled a relatively small but highly capable army of 135,000 men. With Moscow's approval, he began preparations for unifying Korea by force. Neither the Soviets nor the North Koreans expected the United States to oppose the Communists with military forces. Meanwhile the South Koreans—with American advice and assistance—organized a small ground force of about 65,000 troops equipped well enough to prevent border raids and to preserve internal security, but not to fight a hard war. Ready or not, the American and South Korean armed forces were about to be involved in a life and death struggle.

The War Begins

North Korea had completed preparations for an offensive against South Korea by June 23, 1950. The main attack, which was conducted by the 3rd and 4th North Korean divisions, aimed at Seoul on the west coast and began at about 0430 hours on June 25. Farther to the east in the mountains, the 2nd and 7th North Korean divisions drove toward Yoju and Wonju, and on the east coast, the 5th Division (reinforced) headed for Samch'ok. Second echelon regiments followed closely, prepared to attack through the lead units to objectives deep in the South Koreans' rear. Advancing on a broad front, the North Koreans achieved success everywhere. The South Korean forces, which were also known as Republic of Korea (ROK) forces and which were defending along the 38th Parallel, fell back in the face of superior enemy strength, hardly delaying the North Koreans.

As North Korean troops advanced south toward Seoul, President Truman concluded that the United States—as part of a United Nations'

President Truman reports to the nation on the actions taken by the United States. He had earlier stated, "The attack upon Korea makes it plain beyond all doubt that Communism has passed beyond the use of subversion to conquer independent nations and will now use armed invasion and war."

effort—had to oppose communist aggression in the Far East. In a complete reversal of policy, he decided American forces would intervene to save South Korea. Opposition to U.N. involvement came from the communist states, but because the Soviets had walked out of the U.N. Security Council the preceding January, their resistance was uncoordinated and ineffective. On Sunday, June 25, the U.N. Security Council adopted an American-sponsored resolution branding the North Korean attack as a breach of the peace and calling on the North Korean government to cease hostilities and withdraw behind the 38th Parallel. On the following Tuesday, the Security Council approved a follow-on resolution calling on members of the United Nations to help South Korea "repel the armed attack and . . . restore international peace and security in the area." The U.N. Security Council designated the president of the United States as its executive agent for the war in Korea. Truman, in turn, appointed General MacArthur as the Commander-in-Chief, United Nations Command (CINCUNC).

MacArthur's mission was to stop the North Koreans and eject them from South Korea. Somehow he had to slow down the North Koreans sufficiently to give him time to mount a counterattack against their flanks or rear. His first act was to delay what appeared to be the enemy's main attack on the Seoul-Suwon-Ch'onan-Taejon axis leading to the port of Pusan in the south. On the last day of June, MacArthur ordered Major General William F. Dean, commanding general of the 24th Infantry Division, to send an infantry-artillery task force to Korea as the vanguard for the division. The task force—known as Task Force Smith, after Lieutenant Colonel Charles B. Smith, commander of the 1st Battalion, 21st Infantry—consisted of about half the battalion. It reached Taejon on July 2 and moved toward a defensive position about five kilometers north of Osan. Though greatly diminished in strength, the Americans were confident that they could halt the North Koreans. One general officer told Smith, "All we need is some men up there who won't run when they see tanks." By first light on July 5, Colonel Smith's units were in place, and Battery B, 52nd Field Artillery, was prepared to provide fire support.

Beginning around 0700 on July 5, the task force received an attack from North Korean tanks, all of which tried to drive through the American position. About twenty of Smith's infantrymen were killed or wounded in the fight. Damaged but not defeated, with enemy tanks somewhere in its rear, Task Force Smith received another attack several hours later. Attacking frontally, the leading North Korean infantry units took heavy casualties; they then managed to envelop Smith's position and seize high ground on both flanks. Around 1430 hours, Smith decided that his small command had done all it could and ordered his troops to withdraw. As the infantrymen attempted to pull back, enemy pressure increased and prevented some of the Americans from making a fighting withdrawal. A few of them abandoned their crew-served weapons and their rifles. They also left some of their dead and wounded behind. Fortunately for the Americans, the North Koreans chose not to pursue aggressively. The next morning, remnants of Task Force Smith reached Ch'onan. After other survivors made their way back, the final count of missing was 148 soldiers and five officers. Any notion that the North Koreans would pull back at the sight of Americans had disappeared.

Establishing the Pusan Perimeter

Though MacArthur's knowledge of the enemy was incomplete in the first few days of the war, he formulated a broad operational plan containing three clearly identifiable phases. The first was to delay the enemy on his main approach and thereby to buy time needed to rush reinforcements to Korea. The second phase was to defend a toehold on the Korean peninsula to allow the buildup of forces through the port of Pusan. The final phase was an amphibious turning movement by a corps raised in Japan that would strike at the waist of Korea and trap the North Koreans between the new beachhead and Pusan.

For the three-phased operation, MacArthur had advantages in his air and naval forces. Aircraft from the Far East Air Force (FEAF) and the navy soon controlled the sky and provided close air support to Koreans and those few Americans then on the ground. By July 3, Australian air units joined the growing U.N. air force. U.S. carriers launched aircraft to strike targets in North Korea on July 4 and 5. Naval surface forces quickly assembled in Korean waters and secured the sea routes between Japan and Korea. Naval

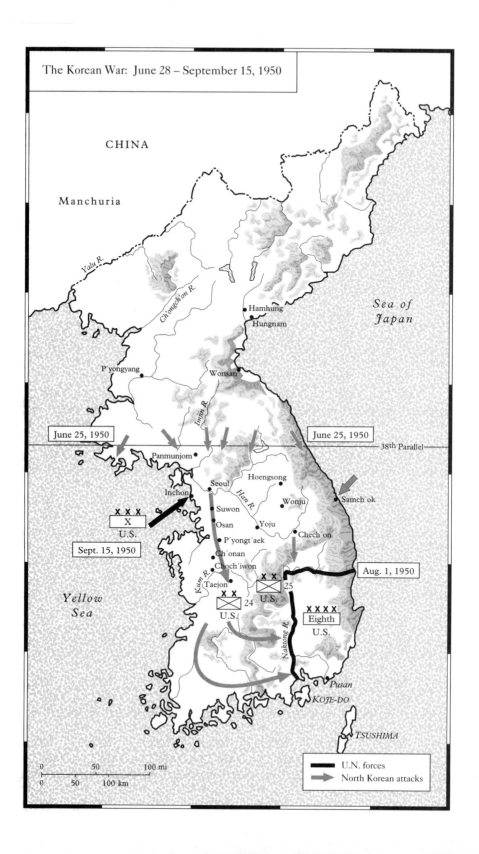

The Korean War: June 28 – September 15, 1950

CHINA

Manchuria

Yalu R.

Ch'ongch'on R.

Hamhung

Hungnam

Sea of Japan

P'yongyang

Wonsan

Imjin R.

June 25, 1950

June 25, 1950

Panmunjom

38th Parallel

Hoengsong

Seoul

Han R.

Inchon

Wonju

Samch'ok

XXX

X

U.S.

Suwon

Osan

Yoju

Sept. 15, 1950

P'yongt'aek

Chech'on

Ch'onan

Choch'iwon

Kum R.

Taejon

XX

25

Aug. 1, 1950

XX

U.S.

Yellow Sea

XX

24

Naktong R.

U.S.

XXXX

Eighth

U.S.

Pusan

KOJE-DO

TSUSHIMA

0   50   100 mi

0   50   100 km

U.N. forces

North Korean attacks

patrols halted the movement of supplies from China and the USSR into North Korea and prevented the infiltration of troops and supplies by sea to the North Koreans south of the 38th Parallel.

U.N. air and naval superiority enabled ground forces to fight numerically superior enemy formations successfully throughout the war. Time and again, even when U.N. forces were in retreat and facing serious setbacks, tactical aircraft and naval gunfire saved the ground forces from being overwhelmed. Beyond the battlefield, supporting aircraft and ships carried war matériel to the combat zone in record-breaking time. The arrival of reinforcements and equipment around the first of August, when Eighth Army and the ROK army were backed into their defensive perimeter around Pusan, saved the whole war effort. Such was the power of air and naval superiority.

In addition to the United States, other members of the United Nations sent forces to aid South Korea. In the end fifty-three nations responded favorably even though actual contributions were slow in coming. Among those sending contingents were Great Britain, Australia, New Zealand, Canada, the Philippines, Sweden, the Netherlands, Belgium, France, Turkey, Thailand, Belgium, Greece, India, and South Africa. Some eventually sent combat forces that played significant roles fighting alongside American regiments.

While the U.N. allies marshaled forces, General Walker and his soldiers in Eighth Army shouldered the crucial task of holding on in Korea long enough to mount the amphibious counteroffensive. The North Koreans proved to be strong, numbering perhaps 80,000 troops and up to 150 tanks. Walker had four U.S. divisions at his disposal—the 7th, 24th, 25th, and the 1st Cavalry Division—but they were spread across the length of Japan and had to be transported to Korea. First he pushed the rest of the 24th Infantry Division into Korea to join Task Force Smith in blocking the enemy's main axis of advance. The division fought the North Koreans in a series of delaying actions at P'yongt'aek and Ch'onan on July 8, at Choch'iwon on the 11th, and on the Kum River between the 13th and 15th. The North Koreans pressed ahead, attacking much as they had against Task Force Smith: advancing along main roads in valleys; striking the American front with tanks, infantry, and artillery; enveloping the flanks with infantry who swarmed across the rugged hills; destroying command posts, supporting artillery, and mortars in the rear; and blocking escape with powerful roadblocks to unnerve the defenders.

When the 25th Division arrived, Walker sent it north to join the 24th in delaying the enemy. To move the 1st Cavalry Division into the country and on line with the 24th and 25th, Walker needed a delay of two days at Taejon. Dean and the 24th Division provided the two days even though they were hopelessly outnumbered. With the 1st Cavalry Division now positioned to its rear, the battered 24th gave up Taejon on July 20 and fell back to the Naktong River. Among its casualties was General Dean, who became engaged in the fight, was cut off, and escaped, only to be captured after weeks of evading the North Koreans. As the enemy continued attacking, Walker slowly gave up ground until his forces were pushed into the

"Pusan Perimeter," as it came to be known. U.S. troops occupied the western part of the defensive perimeter, while the South Koreans covered the northern part.

As reinforcements poured into Pusan and combat strength began to favor Walker, MacArthur assembled forces in Japan for his amphibious operation, now planned for mid-September. Despite the deep concern of the Joint Chiefs of Staff (JCS) for the fate of Eighth Army in the Pusan Perimeter, MacArthur was convinced that his complete superiority of air power and growing strength in tanks, artillery, and infantry would enable Eighth Army and the South Koreans to hold Pusan. His confidence was soon to be tested.

Beginning on August 5 the North Koreans launched violent, piecemeal attacks against the perimeter. Walker parried their thrusts by skillfully shifting his meager reserves between threatened points. Better organized and more savage attacks began on August 31. By this time Walker enjoyed greater combat power, particularly in tanks and artillery. By September 12, the North Korean offensive had spent itself on all fronts against Walker's skillful defense. Best of all, virtually all the enemy's units were concentrated against Pusan. The time for a counteroffensive had arrived.

The Inchon Landing

Though Inchon had the worst physical characteristics that could be imagined in an amphibious objective, MacArthur was convinced that the advantages of seizing it were worth the risk. He believed that the North Koreans, concentrated around the Pusan Perimeter in the south, would be vulnerable to an amphibious turning movement aimed so far to the north. Their vulnerability would be increased because Inchon was so close to the capital city of Seoul. Not only would the capture of Seoul be an important psychological victory, but even more important, Seoul was the intersection of most of the major roads and railroads in South Korea. To capture this intersection would force the North Koreans to surrender or escape to the mountains, abandoning all their heavy equipment.

Detractors of the plan, however, made strong arguments against Inchon as an objective. It had treacherous hydrographic conditions including nine to eleven meter tides, strong tidal currents caused by channel islands, and mud flats that stranded ships at low tide. To gain the most advantage from otherwise difficult tidal conditions, the attack had to begin on September 15. After that the weather turned cold, and rough waters made a landing more hazardous. At best, conditions required a daylight approach past the island of Wolmi-do, which if defended would be a dangerous obstacle. Even worse, a second wave could not follow the first until the next high tide, twelve hours later. Concerns about the defenders at Pusan and the risks inherent in the Inchon landing bothered the Joint Chiefs of Staff and General Walker, as well as some of MacArthur's naval and marine commanders who had to carry it out. Only MacArthur maintained a public air of confidence, so bold that it bordered on arrogance.

Beginning early in September, according to plan, naval air forces struck targets up and down the west coast of Korea; the U.S. Air Force provided general air support farther inland. As the days passed, naval air attacks converged on the Inchon area. Surface gunfire support ships took station off the harbor and began to add their weight. On September 15, Major General Edward M. Almond's X Corps made the amphibious assault at Inchon. The 1st Marine Division made the ship-to-shore landing under the cover of heavy naval gunfire and close air support. Early in the morning, marines took Wolmi-do, and on the next high tide they landed in Inchon north of the Wolmi-do causeway and then fought through the southern edge of the city. The 7th Division landed in Inchon after marines had cleared the city and then moved south of the marines to secure the south bank of the Han River and the high ground between Seoul and Suwon. Though the North Koreans were surprised, they fought fiercely to hold Seoul. Almond's X Corps nevertheless prevailed, and the city fell on September 28.

Despite the landing at Inchon, the heaviest concentration of North Koreans remained around the Pusan Perimeter, and Eighth Army had difficulty breaking out. Finally, a week after X Corps landed at Inchon, the North Koreans began to waver. On September 23, they started a general withdrawal, and Eighth Army units advanced. Within hours, the North Korean withdrawal turned into a rout as enemy soldiers sought refuge across the 38th Parallel or in the mountains of South Korea.

MacArthur's success was largely due to the confidence he had in the strategy and methods employed in the Pacific during World War II. His turning movement at Inchon completely reversed the strategic situation, giving U.N. forces the initiative for the first time. By October 1 he had expelled the aggressors from South Korea. Had nothing happened to change his mission, MacArthur could have counted this battle as a decisive victory. A change in MacArthur's mission, however, soon obliged him to continue the war with new constraints and new methods.

Changing War Aims and a Changing War

Even though the allies had achieved their strategic objectives, the war was not over. In retrospect, the turning point in the Korean War occurred when the allies decided to cross the 38th Parallel, to invade North Korea, and to pursue new strategic objectives. Conventional military wisdom demanded the destruction of the North Korean army to prevent a renewal of its aggression. On September 11—four days before the Inchon landing—President Truman approved MacArthur's pursuing the enemy into North Korea, but he adopted prudent restraints to avoid provoking the Chinese and Soviets. No U.N. troops would enter Manchuria or the USSR, only South Koreans would operate along the international border, and if the Soviets or Chinese intervened before the crossing of the 38th Parallel, the operation would be cancelled. The president also changed the national objective from saving

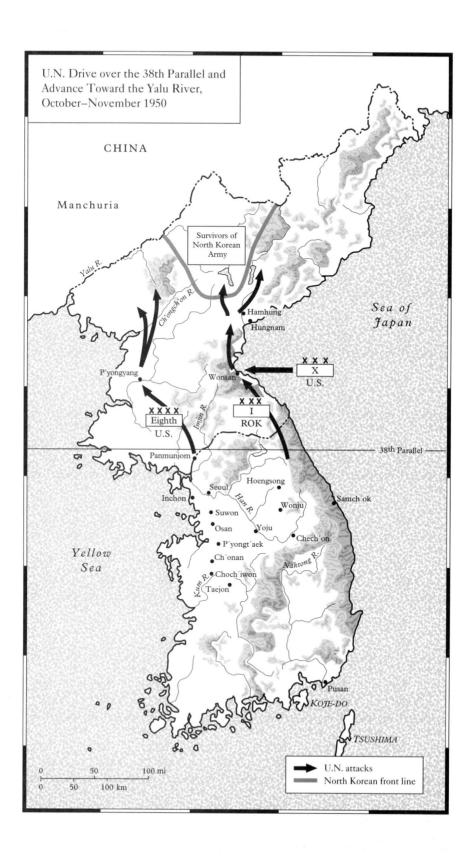

U.N. Drive over the 38th Parallel and
Advance Toward the Yalu River,
October–November 1950

CHINA

Manchuria

Survivors of
North Korean
Army

Yalu R.

Ch'ongch'on R.

Sea of
Japan

Hamhŭng

Hungnam

P'yongyang

Wonsan

X X X
X
U.S.

X X X X
Eighth
U.S.

Imjin R.

X X X
I
ROK

38th Parallel

Panmunjom

Hoengsong

Seoul

Inchon

Suwon

Han R.

Wonju

Samch'ok

Osan

Yoju

Chech'on

P'yongt'aek

Yellow
Sea

Ch'onan

Naktong R.

Kum R.

Choch'iwon

Taejon

Pusan

KOJE-DO

TSUSHIMA

0   50   100 mi
0   50   100 km

➤ U.N. attacks
━ North Korean front line

South Korea to unifying the peninsula. After the United Nations passed a resolution calling for unification of the peninsula on October 7, MacArthur sent his forces into North Korea.

MacArthur's operations in North Korea never achieved the success of his earlier operations. He sent the exhausted Eighth Army in the main attack against the North Korean capital of P'yongyang and mounted a new amphibious assault by X Corps against the east coast port of Wonsan. Although Eighth Army advanced rapidly against light resistance, the amphibious assault by X Corps was six days late because mine sweepers ran into an elaborate mine field. Almost two weeks before the marines could land, Wonsan fell to a South Korean corps that had advanced north along the coast. After the capture of P'yongyang and Wonsan, allied troops streamed north virtually unopposed. In a conference with President Truman at Wake Island on October 15, MacArthur was optimistic about an early victory. Beginning on the 25th, however, a reinvigorated enemy struck Eighth Army and X Corps in a brief but furious counterattack. By November 2, intelligence officers had accumulated undeniable evidence from across the front that Chinese Communist Forces (CCF) from the People's Republic of China had intervened.

Before U.N. forces crossed the 38th Parallel, Chinese leaders had tried to ward off a direct confrontation with the Americans by warning them in September not to cross the 38th Parallel. American leaders interpreted these statements as bluff rather than policy. But they were wrong. Alarmed at the collapse of the North Koreans and concerned about the possible presence of American forces on China's borders, Mao Zedong—the supreme political and military leader of China—received promises of air support from Stalin and decided to intervene. Between October 14 and November 1, some 180,000 Chinese crossed the Yalu River and secretly massed in front of the U.N. Command.

Not knowing the full extent of the Chinese commitment, MacArthur believed their late October attack was a limited gesture rather than a serious intervention. After a three-week delay, while Eighth Army finally replenished its depleted supplies, the U.N. Commander resumed the advance. On November 24 the troops of Eighth Army, supported by an all-out effort by air forces, launched a rapid attack toward the Yalu River. Within twenty-four hours after Eighth Army jumped off, the Chinese struck; they aimed their main attack at the ROK II Corps on the army's right flank. Two days later the CCF hit X Corps as well. Stunned, American and South Korean units recoiled and began a long retreat that did not end until early January 1951.

Effective close air support enabled MacArthur's ground forces to escape. For days at a time, air forces were the only U.N. opposition to the advancing enemy. Timely and accurate attacks by relays of fighter bombers stopped the enemy in front of U.N. defenders. The Chinese, in their haste to close with Eighth Army in the west, abandoned their habitual concealment and marched night and day along primary and secondary roads. Casualties among men and vehicles from air attacks mounted so high that Chinese commanders had to confine road movement to nighttime, thus slowing the advance significantly. As the troops of Eighth Army put some distance

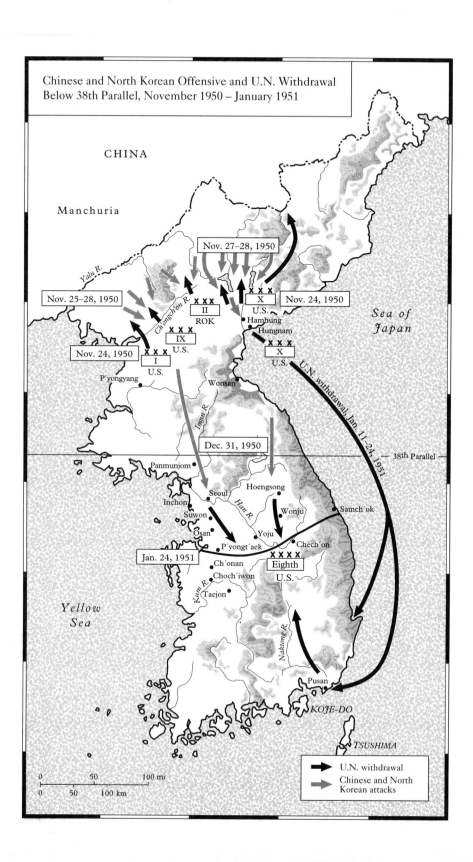

Chinese and North Korean Offensive and U.N. Withdrawal
Below 38th Parallel, November 1950 – January 1951

CHINA

Manchuria

Nov. 27–28, 1950

Nov. 25–28, 1950

Yalu R.

Ch'ongch'on R.

X X X
II
ROK

X X X
X
U.S.

Nov. 24, 1950

Hamhung

Hungnam

X X X
IX
U.S.

X X X
I
U.S.

Nov. 24, 1950

X X X
X
U.S.

Sea of Japan

P'yongyang

Wonsan

Imjin R.

Dec. 31, 1950

U.N. withdrawal Jan. 11–24, 1951

38th Parallel

Panmunjom

Seoul

Hoengsong

Inchon

Han R.

Wonju

Samch'ok

Suwon

Osan

Yoju

Chech'on

P'yongt'aek

X X X X
Eighth
U.S.

Jan. 24, 1951

Ch'onan

Choch'iwon

Kum R.

Taejon

Yellow Sea

Naktong R.

Pusan

KOJE-DO

TSUSHIMA

| 0 | 50 | 100 mi |
| 0 | 50 | 100 km |

➤ U.N. withdrawal

➤ Chinese and North Korean attacks

between themselves and the Chinese, the air forces attacked and destroyed Chinese supplies and equipment. Then in mid-December FEAF launched a coordinated interdiction campaign against railway yards and bridges, highway bridges, tunnels, and supply dumps. Eighth Army owed its survival and subsequent resurgence in January 1951 to overwhelming air support during its retreat.

Defeat in North Korea forced the United Nations to reexamine its war aims in light of Chinese involvement. MacArthur quickly charged that he was facing "an entirely new war" and that the strategy for war against North Korea did not apply in a war against China. MacArthur wanted more forces and a broader charter to retaliate against the Chinese. But even in the darkest days before the Inchon landing, American leaders believed that restraint was necessary to avoid widening the war. Within the broader scope of the Cold War, Europe remained the main concern of American policy, not Asia; attacks on China could bring on Soviet involvement and even expand the war to Europe. MacArthur's proposals to increase his forces and to retaliate against the Chinese were therefore completely at odds with those of his president and other U.N. leaders.

During the first week of December, when reports from the front were grim, President Truman met Prime Minister Clement R. Attlee of the United Kingdom in Washington. Attlee had flown to the United States after Truman had hinted publicly that atomic weapons might be used in Korea. Speaking for some other U.N. members, he questioned American direction

Chinese soldiers proved tough, skillful, and numerous. To neutralize U.N. advantages in fire power, they advanced by stealth and infiltration and often attacked at night while making wild bugle calls and barbaric screams. They steadily increased their artillery, firing a record of more than 93,000 rounds on one day in October 1952.

of the war. His principal interest was to induce the Chinese to stop fighting and withdraw. Truman entered the talks committed to sticking it out in Korea and even continuing the war against China if forced off the peninsula. Initially the two allies could not have been farther apart. After four days of intense discussions, however, the two reached a compromise solution: they would continue to fight side by side in Korea, find a line and hold it, and wait for an opportunity to negotiate an end to the fighting from a position of military strength. Moreover, they reaffirmed their commitment to "Europe first" in the face of Soviet hostility toward NATO. In essence the decision to unify Korea was abrogated and a new war aim adopted.

Significantly, the most immediate military effect of the talks was to prevent MacArthur from exacting revenge for his humiliating defeat. The Joint Chiefs limited his reinforcements to replacements, shifted the priority of military resources to strengthening NATO forces, and wrote a new directive for MacArthur that required him to defend in Korea as far to the north as possible. MacArthur was outraged. He disagreed with giving priority to Europe at the expense of the shooting war in Korea. He smoldered at the thought of going on the strategic defensive and fought determinedly against the new directive. Nevertheless, on January 12, 1951, the JCS sent him the final version of the order to conduct a strategic defensive. In essence, U.N. forces had a new war aim designed to bring about a negotiated settlement.

Ridgway's War

Just two days before Christmas in 1950, the command of Eighth Army passed to Lieutenant General Matthew B. Ridgway after General Walker died when a Korean truck hit his jeep. Ridgway arrived at his new headquarters determined to halt the retreat and to attack north as soon as possible. Somehow he had to reunite X Corps with Eighth Army, stop the retreat, and turn the army around. He also had to revive the fighting spirit of his troops.

General Douglas MacArthur and General Matthew B. Ridgway. Ridgway carefully tailored operations to correct the problems of Eighth Army. His self-assurance and his success soon restored the confidence of Eighth Army.

One of the immediate problems he faced was the separation of X Corps in Hungnam on the east coast from Eighth Army on the western flank. As Eighth Army fell back, the gap between the two forces increased, and on December 13, X Corps was evacuated by sea from Hungnam. As Eighth Army continued falling back, Ridgway's American I and IX Corps held the western sector, while a ROK Corps held the eastern end of the line. Two other ROK corps stretched themselves over the extended mountainous center. Unfortunately for the U.N. forces, Chinese and North Korean units could easily penetrate the center in a southwesterly direction and force Eighth Army to move farther south to avoid being trapped in the Seoul area by having its right flank enveloped or turned. The difficulties of this tactical situation had plagued Walker, and now, even as FEAF conducted a furious five-day air assault to halt the enemy's advance, a Chinese and North Korean penetration forced Ridgway to give up Seoul and fall below a line between Osan and Samch'ok (on the east coast).

After Ridgway pulled back, his front-line units reported only light contact with the enemy, leading him to conclude that Chinese units were unable to maintain pressure. Sensing the opportunity to turn on the Chinese, Ridgway halted on a line from P'yongt'aek in the west to Samch'ok on the east coast. When American divisions, withdrawn from Hungnam with X Corps, moved up to thicken the line in the lightly held center, Ridgway ordered his forces to patrol north and find the enemy. His offensive campaign began with an attack by the tank-supported 27th Regimental Combat Team on January 15. He next sent IX Corps units toward Inchon on the 22nd. An attack by I and IX Corps units then aimed north of Suwon and Yoju toward the Han River on the 25th. By February 10, I Corps had reached the Han River and captured Inchon and Kimp'o Airfield near Seoul.

Ridgway now looked to X Corps in the central sector to drive north against Wonju and Hoengsong. Although X Corps enjoyed early success, two CCF armies and a North Korean corps attacked south through gaps in the ROK sector to the east. They broke through three ROK divisions and forced X Corps to withdraw to Wonju. As the enemy attempted once again to drive southwest, bitter fighting raged around Wonju and Chip'yongni, the southern and northern shoulders of the penetration. Ridgway filled the gap between the two towns, defenders held the shoulders by heroic sacrifice, and the U.N. command defeated the enemy attack.

In what amounted to a renewal of his previous attack, Ridgway sent IX and X Corps north in Operation "Killer" on February 21. After Chinese and North Korean pressure subsided along the new front stretching from Chip'yongni southeastward through Wonju to Chech'on, extensive patrolling by U.N. forces disclosed that the enemy was pulling back from the salient created by their attack. Patrols reported bits of information that painted a fairly convincing picture of an army badly in need of reorganization and resupply. Though intelligence officers could not account for all the enemy forces in Korea, they nonetheless identified five Chinese armies and three North Korean corps in front of the allies. Ridgway judged the potential gains of a quick offensive to be worth the risks of an incomplete intelligence picture. He believed a rapid resumption of the U.N. offensive would take

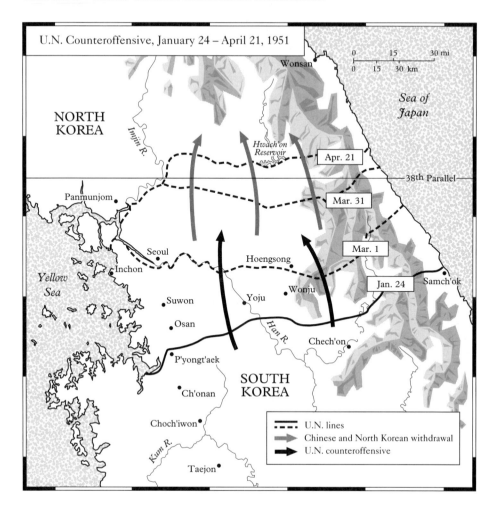

advantage of the weakened condition of the Chinese and North Korean soldiers and inflict a large number of casualties.

Ridgway's plan included an objective line known as Arizona, that ran
from Yangp'yong on the Han River, to north of Chip'yongni and Wonju, and
then to Kangnung on the east coast. Line Arizona was about twenty kilometers north of the U.N. front lines. The main effort would move along two
axes of advance, the westernmost by U.S. IX Corps, aiming from Wonju
north to Hoengsong. In the eastern sector, U.S. X Corps was to attack north
to a road junction just south of Line Arizona and then attack west across the
corps front to block further enemy withdrawal. The west flank of the attack
was to be protected by U.S. I Corps and the east flank by the ROK III
Corps. In all, eight American and ROK divisions and a British brigade
would comprise the attacking force, and the rest of the army would support.
The operation was code-named Killer to emphasize its main purpose.

Ridgway wanted Eighth Army units to learn from the mistakes of
previous operations. He warned corps commanders to maintain tight contact between adjacent frontline units and to avoid the gaps that had doomed

South Koreans poured forth by the thousands to repel the invaders, but they initially performed poorly because of inexperienced leaders and inadequate training. Not until entire ROK divisions were withdrawn from the lines and sent through training programs did they become—to use Ridgway's words—"first rate fighting forces."

the previous attack. He wanted units to advance along the high ground and envelope enemy positions rather than assault them frontally. As was his custom in Korea, Ridgway saw the ground advance as a series of short, methodical steps, controlled by phase lines and characterized by heavy air and artillery fire on enemy positions before the infantry advanced.

Operation Killer began precisely as planned before dawn on February 21, except for one unforeseeable event. Up to that day, snow had covered the ground, roads were frozen hard, and rivers and streams were covered with thick ice. On the 21st, the temperature soared to 50 degrees Fahrenheit and remained above freezing during daylight for the rest of the month. The falling snow became rain, the ground thawed, roads turned into deep mud, melting snow filled streambeds, and breaking ice rushed downstream destroying bridges and making fords impassable. Each night the surface froze again, only to melt at sunup. Thus Operation Killer, conceived as a rapid strike to cut off enemy forces, became a plodding advance at a speed dictated by nature.

U.N. forces advanced toward Line Arizona against scattered delaying forces left behind by the enemy. By the end of February, Ridgway had made significant gains but could not catch the enemy. As the two corps labored forward, rain, mud, and high water became the real enemies. The 1st Marine Division of IX Corps finally reached the hills overlooking Hoengsong, and the 7th Infantry Division of X Corps turned west to begin sweeping across the corps front. By March 6 all the objectives had been achieved. Though the infantry of Eighth Army never closed decisively with the enemy, forward units found heavy casualties littering the hills and buried in shallow graves; most were attributable to intense artillery fire and close air support.

On March 7, Ridgway launched another carefully controlled attack. When U.S. forces crossed the Han River east of Seoul, the CCF abandoned the capital; allied forces continued moving north. In early April the U.N. advance slowed as units prepared strong defensive positions in anticipation of an enemy counteroffensive. Surprisingly, the shock came not from the enemy as expected but from Washington when Truman dismissed MacArthur.

The Relief of MacArthur

One way to view MacArthur's relief is to consider it as the last step necessary to adapt the war effort to the new war aims. MacArthur bristled under the new directive requiring him to defend South Korea rather than rebuild an offensive capability to unify the peninsula. With his outrage so close to the surface, it was only a matter of time before he gave the president good reason to dismiss him.

MacArthur had been a difficult subordinate. He had clashed with Truman over U.S. policy toward Formosa early in the war and complained about the restrictions placed on his forces and his freedom to wage the war. Occasionally he had been uncommunicative with the JCS. Then after the retreat of Eighth Army, he publicly suggested that the policies of the Truman administration had been responsible for the defeat. Truman was angered by this charge, and on December 6, 1950, he published an executive order—aimed at MacArthur—requiring all government officials to clear their public statements on foreign and military policy with the administration. Mac-Arthur then objected to the JCS directive of January 12, 1951, written to implement the Truman-Attlee agreements. By requiring MacArthur to go on the defensive, that directive squelched any hope of unifying the peninsula and defeating the Chinese and North Koreans. In February and again in March, MacArthur called for a new strategy, presumably one that would permit him to attack the Chinese in their sanctuary north of the Yalu River.

As Ridgway neared the 38th Parallel again, a position of military strength seemed near at hand. President Truman took advantage of Ridgway's success to invite the Communists to negotiate a cease-fire. After reading the text of Truman's proposed message, MacArthur broadcast a bellicose ultimatum to the enemy commander undermining the president's plan. Truman was furious; MacArthur had preempted presidential prerogative, confused friends and enemies alike about who was directing the war, and directly challenged the president's authority as commander-in-chief. As Truman pondered how to handle the problem, Congressman Joseph W. Martin, Minority (Republican) Leader of the House of Representatives, released the contents of a letter from MacArthur in which the general repeated his criticism of the administration. The next day Truman began the process that was to end with MacArthur's relief from command on April 11.

Ending the War: Politics as War

After MacArthur's relief, Ridgway took his place as Commander-in-Chief, Far East and CINCUNC. Lieutenant General James A. Van Fleet, an experienced and successful World War II combat leader, took command of the Eighth Army. On April 22, as Van Fleet's army edged north, the CCF opened the expected general offensive, aiming their main attack toward Seoul in the west. The Chinese, numbering almost a half-million men, drove the U.N. defenders south. Followed closely by this formidable force, Van Fleet had to withdraw once again below the 38th Parallel, finally halting a bare eight kilometers north of Seoul.

On May 10 the Chinese jumped off again, this time concentrating seven armies in their main effort in the east-central and eastern sector of the U.N. line. They drove X Corps and two ROK corps south of the 38th Parallel

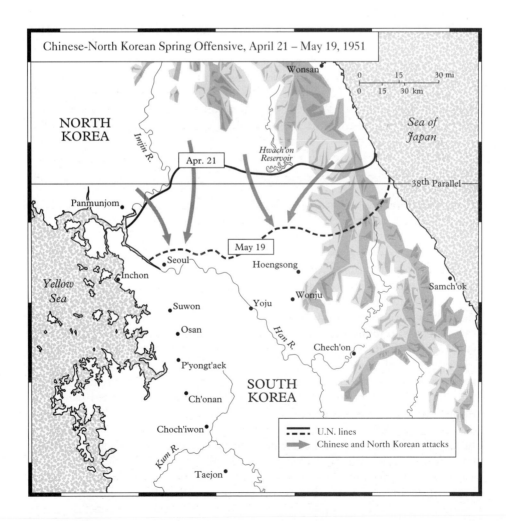

Chinese-North Korean Spring Offensive, April 21 – May 19, 1951

but paid a heavy price for thinning their front in the west. Taking advantage of the Chinese concentration in the east, Van Fleet attacked suddenly in the west, north of Seoul. The rest of the Eighth Army attacked to the front. The effect was dramatic; surprised CCF units pulled back, suffering their heaviest casualties of the war, and by the end of May found themselves retreating into North Korea. By mid-June 1951, U.N. forces had regained a line, for the most part north of the 38th Parallel. There they remained. The yearlong mobile phase of the Korean War had ended, and a strange war in which most battles were fought over the control of outposts between front lines had begun. The outpost war would continue for the next two years.

Negotiations and Stalemate

Regardless of U.N. success on the battlefield, ending the war turned out to be a maddeningly long process. U.S. planners knew that because of the Truman-Attlee agreement, the war would probably not end in a conventional victory. Obtaining a cease-fire had become an implicit war aim of the United Nations. Moreover, Chinese and North Korean commanders needed a respite from the heavy casualties sustained in Van Fleet's recent offensive. Consequently both sides agreed in late June 1951 to begin negotiations. The subsequent negotiations were initially hampered by haggling over matters of protocol and the selection of a truly neutral site. On July 26, 1951, the two sides finally agreed on an agenda containing four major points: fixing a demarcation line and demilitarized zone, supervising the truce, handling prisoners of war, and making recommendations to the governments involved in the war. With an agenda in hand, negotiators at Panmunjom began the lengthy process of debating each item. Meanwhile, the fighting continued.

After receiving reinforcements in early summer, Van Fleet conducted limited attacks to strengthen his defensive line and keep pressure on the Communists. All across the front, divisions sent combat teams forward to capture key terrain features. By the end of October, Van Fleet had a new and more commanding line that provided tactical advantage to Eighth Army. He wanted to continue his attacks, but Ridgway directed him to stop and carry on an "active defense." At stake was the success of negotiations aimed at establishing a demarcation line.

On November 17 the U.N. delegation presented the Communists with a proposal to designate the current line of contact as the demarcation line, provided that all remaining agenda items were resolved within thirty days. The allies believed this proposal would make possible an early resolution of differences and a quick end to the war. But it also provided the Communists a windfall opportunity, for they could negotiate the agenda items while strengthening their defensive positions. At the end of the thirty days, the U.N. would have no agreement and would face a defensive zone too formidable to crack with the forces at hand. The communist negotiators accepted the proposal on November 27; on December 27 the United Nations faced an enemy defensive line so deeply dug in that both sides had to accept a stalemate. From that moment on, the battlefield regressed to a static kind of war, reminiscent of World War I.

As ground action waned, the United Nations turned to powerful air and naval arms for military pressure to support its negotiating team. In August 1951, air, naval, and marine commanders concentrated all available aircraft on the interdiction of Communist-controlled bridges, highways, railroad lines and yards, and supply points. Most of the air assets took part in Operation "Strangle," a road and rail-cutting scheme designed to slow down the southward movement of enemy troops and matériel. Operation "Saturate," which followed Strangle, placed even greater emphasis on the railway-interdiction effort. During the day, fighter-bombers raked the railroad lines; at night, B-26s scoured the countryside for trucks. Approximately ninety-six fighter sorties a day continued to provide close air support to the ground war. Despite the heavy bombing, enemy work details devised ingenious ways to repair the railroad overnight. The North Korean Railroad Bureau employed three brigades full time on railroad repair and, at the height of the air campaign, used as many as 500,000 soldiers and civilians to keep the lines open. The sustained bombing campaign also forced the communist air forces out of their Manchurian sanctuary in an attempt to stop interdiction of roads and rail lines. Beginning in September 1951, communist MiG-15s became more aggressive and more numerous—as many as ninety at a time entered North Korean airspace—bringing an end to the allies' uncontested control of the air. When communist fighters chose to challenge U.N. aircraft, however, they suffered heavy losses.

Beginning in May 1952, the United Nations used air power more forcefully to place greater pressure on the Communists. Despite numerous attacks on supply centers, transportation networks, and personnel, neither the North Koreans nor the Chinese acceded to the U.N. armistice terms; on the contrary, both became more intransigent and refused to yield to such pressure. As a result, aerial bombing added to the Communists' difficulties but it did not succeed in driving them from the war.

Achieving a Cease-Fire

After the winter of 1951–1952, the war in Korea became a seemingly endless succession of violent fire fights, most of them at night, to gain or maintain control of hills that were a little higher and ridges that were a bit straighter. Sharp fighting occurred over places with such names as Pork Chop Hill, Sniper's Ridge, Old Baldy, T-Bone, White Horse, and a hundred other hilltops between the two armies. In some cases, both sides piled on reinforcements until "terrain grabs" turned into prolonged and bloody fights. All of them, no matter how large the forces engaged, were deadly encounters designed to provide leverage for one side or the other in the protracted political war going on at Panmunjom. In an era when technology provided great mobility, tactical warfare in Korea went through a regression that can be explained only in terms of its close relationships to the negotiations. Constant pressure was its purpose, not victory on the battlefield. Pressure in such a stalemated war proved difficult for a democracy to maintain.

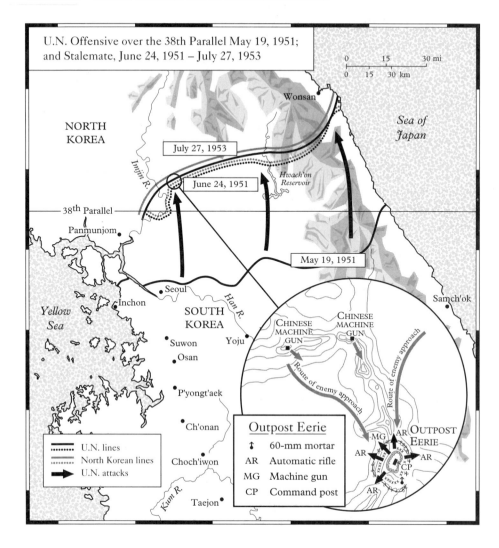

U.N. Offensive over the 38th Parallel May 19, 1951; and Stalemate, June 24, 1951 – July 27, 1953

Outpost Eerie, a battle fought in March 1952, is a good example of a small-unit action typical of the fighting during the stalemate. Eerie was located on the southernmost hilltop on a T-bone shaped complex of ridges and hills. The Chinese held the top of the "T," about 1.5 kilometers to the north of Eerie. The Americans on Outpost Eerie came from Company K, 179th Infantry Regiment, 45th Infantry Division. They normally occupied the hill with two rifle squads, a light machine gun, a 60-mm mortar, and a platoon command group. Supporting fires came from .50-caliber machine guns on the main line of resistance, mortars from the K Company weapons platoon, and artillery from a direct-support battalion. To strengthen their position, the Americans on Eerie dug trenches, built bunkers, and encircled their position with three barbed-wire fences.

Lieutenant Omer Manley's 3rd Platoon of Company K occupied the outpost on March 21. At about 2300 hours, Manley received reports of the Chinese setting up a machine gun on a hill about 600 meters from Eerie. An

American patrol also encountered a platoon-sized enemy formation moving south. After two trip flares went off, the Chinese poured machine-gun fire onto the American position and began trying to break through the wire in two places. Lieutenant Manley called for artillery support and illuminating rounds, while his soldiers fired at the oncoming Chinese. By 0100 hours, the Americans had run out of illuminating rounds, and the Chinese had breached the wire. The Chinese seized the north end of the outpost and advanced across the top of the bunkers. The Americans were pushed to the southern end of the position and soon ran out of ammunition. Manley disappeared after throwing his empty carbine at a Chinese soldier.

At 0120 hours, communications with Eerie ended, and the commander of Company K called for artillery concentrations directly on the outpost. As soon as the artillery firing began, the Chinese withdrew. Company K then advanced to clear the outpost and search for survivors. Of the twenty-six men in Eerie, eight were dead, four wounded, and two missing. Manley could not be found. After discovering thirty-one enemy bodies inside and around the position, Company K repaired the defenses of the outpost and prepared to defend it against the next attack.

As fights such as the one at Outpost Eerie continued nightly, negotiators in Panmunjom plodded through the remaining agenda items. Results came slowly. One extremely contentious issue pertained to the supervision of the armistice agreement. Ridgway wanted an armistice commission with free access to all of Korea and an agreement to ban reinforcement of men and matériel. The Communists countered with a proposal that denied free access and contained no provision for reinforcements or replacements of any kind. Finally a compromise emerged that permitted rotation of 35,000 troops and supplies each month through specified ports of entry. Both sides accepted Swedish, Swiss, Polish, and Czech membership on an armistice commission. The last agenda item on political recommendations was settled quickly; both sides called for a conference to convene three months after a cease-fire. All political issues not settled during the negotiations would be discussed at that conference.

What to do about prisoners of war became the final obstacle to an agreement to end the war. Fearing mistreatment by the Communists, the U.N. Command wanted prisoners to decide for themselves whether or not they would return home. The Communists insisted on forced repatriation as was called for in the Geneva Convention. To restore movement to the talks, the U.N. delegation proposed that prisoners be polled by the International Red Cross about where they wanted to go. The Chinese and North Koreans agreed. When the Red Cross made interim results of the screening known early in April 1952, the data surprised everyone. Of 132,000 Chinese and North Korean prisoners screened, only 54,000 North Koreans and 5,100 Chinese wanted to go home. The communist delegation was incredulous and accused the United Nations of influencing the poll. From that moment on, negotiations bogged down on the prisoner-of-war issue.

At about this same time, May 1952, General Ridgway left Tokyo to become Supreme Allied Commander, Europe. General Mark Clark, who

A U.S. rifle squad attacks. As the stalemate continued, fighting often degenerated into clashes between patrols. Eighth Army sometimes conducted raids by concentrating artillery and air strikes and then sending in small ground forces against the enemy.

had made his reputation during World War II in Italy, replaced Ridgway as CINCUNC. Ridgway's last problem, and Clark's first, was to settle an uprising by hard-core prisoners on Koje-do, an island off the coast of South Korea. In an attempt to derail screening of all prisoners, leaders inside the prisons deliberately provoked their guards. Their crowning success was capturing the camp commander in an unguarded moment and forcing him to terminate forcible screening and to negotiate for humane treatment of prisoners. The Communists trumpeted acceptance of these terms as an admission of inhumane treatment and tampering with the Red Cross poll. Clark was furious and relieved the camp commander. After being reinforced with combat troops, the new camp commander stormed the compounds with tank-infantry teams and isolated the hard-core communist leaders in separate compounds.

The Koje-do incident hurt the negotiating position of the U.N. delegation. Friends, enemies, and neutrals decried the violent suppression of the prisoners, and communist negotiators became intractable on the prisoner-of-war issue. Over the summer of 1952, the language of negotiation became more abusive and inflammatory. Clark had had enough. In exasperation, he ordered the U.N. delegation to walk out of Panmunjom on October 8. With no one to refute their assertions, the Communists gained a major political victory and hammered away at U.N. treatment of prisoners and alleged U.N. violations of the neutral zones surrounding the negotiating site.

Early in 1953 the newly elected president, Dwight D. Eisenhower, increased pressure on the Communists. He believed that the Truman strategy was the only practical one but also believed that something had to be done to give the Communists an incentive to reach agreement. He permitted the air force to bomb dams in North Korea and to flood the countryside. He instructed the JCS to prepare plans for more intensive and mobile battles should negotiations break down. He deployed atomic delivery aircraft to the Far East and ordered them to train for low-level attacks with atomic bombs. And he let it be known that the United States was prepared to renew the war at a higher level unless progress was made at Panmunjom. As the Americans signaled their intentions to expand the war, the death of Joseph Stalin on March 5, 1953, brought on a deadly power struggle in the Kremlin that probably focused Soviet leaders' attention on internal problems rather than a prolonged war. With economic problems adding to political and military concerns, communist leaders in the Soviet Union, China, and North Korea had sufficient reasons to question the continuation of the war.

On March 28, 1953, China and North Korea agreed to an exchange of sick and wounded prisoners and suggested that this might lead to settlement of the entire prisoner-of-war issue and a cease-fire. On April 20, 684 Americans returned to U.N. control and 5,194 North Koreans, 1,030

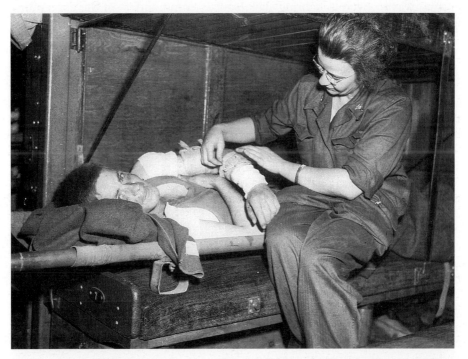

An army nurse providing care to a soldier. With its helicopters, radio dispatch system, and treatment facilities, the Mobile Army Surgical Hospital (MASH) provided better medical care than what had been available in previous wars.

Chinese, and 447 civilians went over to the communist authorities. On April 26, negotiating sessions resumed at Panmunjom. In the following months, negotiators agreed that repatriation was to be offered to all prisoners and that those who chose not to return home were to be turned over to a neutral commission that would hold them for interview by their respective country-men before releasing them.

While the United Nations worked diligently toward an armistice, Syngman Rhee, the South Korean president, became obstructive; he had long demanded the withdrawal of the Chinese from the Korean peninsula and the disarming of the North Korean army. On the night of June 18, Rhee ordered his guards on the prisons to release the friendly North Koreans. During the hours of darkness, 25,000 prisoners disappeared, absorbed into South Korean society. Though Eisenhower was outraged, he convinced Rhee not to undermine the armistice.

As the final details of the agreement were negotiated, the Commu-nists sought one last military advantage. Their goal was to mount an offen-sive that would end at the same time that the truce agreement was signed, thus giving the illusion of a peaceful settlement following a communist vic-tory. They sought to straighten the line in front of the ROK II Corps. Ter-rain objectives were limited to outpost hills in adjacent American sectors. The attacks began against the ROK II Corps on June 10, and by June 16 the U.N. line had been pushed 4,000 meters south. Eighth Army reinforced the ROK II Corps sector for a counterattack, but it was too late. Although some ground was recovered, fighting slackened as commanders of the contending armies prepared to sign the truce.

On July 27, 1953, Mark Clark signed the armistice documents to end the fighting in the Korean War.

☆   ☆   ☆   ☆

For a war intended to be limited, the Korean War exacted a staggering human toll. Although CCF and North Korean casualties are unknown, esti-mates of total losses range between 1.5 and 2 million, plus perhaps 1 million civilians. The U.N. Command suffered a total of 88,000 killed, of whom 23,300 were American. Total casualties for the U.N. (killed, wounded, miss-ing) were 459,360; of these 300,000 were South Korean. For decades after the war, the two armies continued watching each other over the demilita-rized zone and waiting for the day when fighting might begin again.

Until the outbreak of the Korean War, the Cold War had been waged mainly with economic, political, and psychological weapons. War in Korea, however, redefined the conflict between the United States and the Soviet Union as a much more dangerous contest in the nuclear age. Virtually all international incidents thereafter became crises that had the potential for global consequences. No inhabited region of the world was exempt. The antagonists and their allies in NATO and the Warsaw Pact armed themselves and enlisted other states to take sides.

Not surprisingly, after five years of minimal spending for defense, the Korean War also changed the military policy of the United States. Out went austerity as big defense budgets permanently rearmed American as well as allied forces. The war increased the number of U.S. military forces stationed overseas, particularly in Europe. It fostered a peacetime selective service system, the largest standing military force in the nation's history, and the growth of an unprecedented military-scientific-industrial alliance that greatly influenced the world economy thereafter. And it created effective military readiness aimed at going to war with little or no warning.

Perhaps most important in the history of warfare, Korea became a model for limited war and demonstrated alternative ways of gaining national objectives without resorting to atomic war. For the United States, it had been a war limited in scope and violence and fought for alliance objectives. For the communist forces, it had been a war that relied on prolonged armistice negotiations to gain what could not be gained on the battlefield. Thus the significance of the Korean War is less about changes in the technical methods of waging war than about the difficulties and complexities of attaining political goals through the use of military force.

SUGGESTED READINGS

Appleman, Roy E. *South to the Naktong, North to the Yalu, June-November 1950* (Washington, D. C.: Government Printing Office, 1961).

Clark, Mark W. *From the Danube to the Yalu* (New York: Harper, 1954).

Collins, J. Lawton. *War in Peacetime: The History and Lessons of Korea* (Boston: Houghton Mifflin, 1969).

Foot, Rosemary. *A Substitute for Victory: The Politics of Peacemaking at the Korean Armistice Talks* (Ithaca, N.Y.: Cornell University Press, 1990).

Futrell, Robert F. *The United States Air Force in Korea, 1950-1953* (Washington, D.C.: Government Printing Office, 1983).

Goodrich, Leland M. *Korea: A Study of U.S. Policy in the United Nations* (New York: Council on Foreign Relations, 1956).

Goulden, Joseph C. *Korea: The Untold Story of the War* (New York: Times Books, 1982).

Hermes, Walter G. *Truce Tent and Fighting Front* (Washington, D.C.: Government Printing Office, 1966).

Kaufman, Burton I. *The Korean War: Challenges in Crisis, Credibility, and Command* (New York: Knopf, 1986).

Marshall, S. L. A. *The River and the Gauntlet* (New York: Morrow, 1953).

Mossman, Billy C. *Ebb and Flow, November 1950–July 1951* (Washington, D.C.: Government Printing Office, 1990).

Rees, David. *Korea: The Limited War* (New York: St. Martin's Press, 1964).

Ridgway, Matthew B. *The Korean War* (Garden City, N.Y.: Doubleday, 1967).

Schnabel, James F. *Policy and Direction, The First Year* (Washington, D.C.: Government Printing Office, 1972).

3

THE VIETNAM WAR, 1961–1975: REVOLUTIONARY AND CONVENTIONAL WARFARE IN AN ERA OF LIMITED WAR

Vietnam and "People's War"

The United States:
Counterinsurgency
and Limited War

Escalation and Stalemate,
1965–1968

The Tet Offensive, 1968

Fighting While Negotiating,
1968–1975

$\mathbb{T}$he war in Vietnam represented a clash between two very different types of warfare. Fought on the Indochinese peninsula during the years 1961–1975, a direct offshoot of the Cold War, it matched the "revolutionary war" techniques of North Vietnam and the National Liberation Front of South Vietnam (NLF) insurgents against the limited war doctrines and modern, high-technology conventional forces of the United States and its South Vietnamese ally. Militarily, the two sides fought to a prolonged and bloody stalemate. As a consequence, the political dimensions of the war ultimately proved decisive. As long as the North Vietnamese and NLF did not lose, they won, and they successfully employed a protracted war strategy to take advantage of American impatience. Unwilling to expand the war to win in the traditional sense, the United States could do no better than a stalemate, and the war's increasing unpopularity at home eventually forced a U.S. military withdrawal. The United States' military power had never been able to compensate for the political weakness of its client government, and when the United States withdrew, the Saigon regime collapsed in the face of a full-scale North Vietnamese invasion. Whether the war validated North Vietnam's revolutionary war doctrines remains very much in doubt in light of the end of the Cold War. It did prove the difficulty of fighting a limited war in the Cold War setting, and it provoked a major reconsideration of U.S. military doctrine, the outcome of which also remains quite uncertain.

Vietnam and "People's War"

During their thirty-year war against France and the United States the Vietnamese applied a concept variously labeled "People's War" or "Revolutionary War." The Vietnamese approach to warfare was multifaceted, combining military, political, and diplomatic measures in a tightly integrated manner. Even in the military realm, it involved guerrilla warfare as well as more conventional methods. The Vietnamese relied especially on a mobilized citizenry and the application of a protracted war strategy, and in both their wars with France and the United States, they counted on wearing down less patient enemies fighting unpopular wars far from their shores.

A Martial Tradition

The Vietnamese drew on a rich military tradition that was an essential part of their heritage. For roughly one thousand years, the land of Nam Viet (later Vietnam) was the southernmost province of China. During much of that time, the Vietnamese had fiercely resisted the domination of their larger northern neighbor. Perhaps the most famous of Vietnamese heroes, the Trung sisters, mounted elephants to lead the first major rebellion against a much superior Chinese force and, when defeated, drowned themselves in a lake in Hanoi. Another woman, Trieu Au, led yet another unsuccessful revolt in 248 A.D. In the tenth century the Vietnamese won their independence by luring an attacking Chinese fleet into a river bed in which they had planted iron-tipped spikes, impaling the ships of the invaders.

In the thirteenth century, the Vietnamese repulsed the legendary Mongol warrior Kublai Khan three times. Using the inhospitable climate and terrain to advantage, their leader, Tran Hung Dao, pioneered methods of guerrilla warfare later used against the French and Americans, avoiding head-on engagements and employing hit-and-run tactics to exhaust a stronger enemy. In his *Essential Summary of Military Arts*, Dao observed that "The enemy must fight his battles far from his home base for a long time. . . . We must further weaken him by drawing him into protracted campaigns. Once his initial dash is broken, it will be easier to destroy him." In the climactic battle against the Mongols in the Red River Valley in 1287, the Vietnamese defeated three hundred thousand enemy troops. Finally, in 1426, another legendary figure, Le Loi, defeated the Chinese and secured independence for Vietnam.

The years of resistance to China and the victories over the Mongols comprise an essential part of Vietnamese folklore. "Through the millennia of their history the Vietnamese people have struggled incessantly against foreign invaders . . . in great battles that took place one century after another," a contemporary history observes. In their own mythology, the Vietnamese repeatedly win against stronger enemies through cleverness, ingenuity, and virtue, and because of their ability to mobilize all the people, to make every citizen a soldier. "We fight and win . . . because we are . . . moral, loyal, patient, strong, indomitable, filled with compassion," Communist party chief Le Duan told soldiers during the American war. "We have been fighting for our independence for four thousand years," Premier Pham Van Dong warned the Americans through two French emissaries in 1967. "We have defeated the Mongols three times. The United States Army, strong as it is, is not as terrifying as Genghis [sic] Khan."

Although it is less celebrated by the Vietnamese, expansion to the south forms as important a part of their military heritage as resistance to northern invaders. After defeating the Mongols, they moved southward to conquer the kingdom of Champa and after nearly two centuries of fighting destroyed its capital of Indrapura and killed 40,000 people. National unity was always a fragile matter, however, and civil war continued until the French imposed peace on Vietnam through colonization.

Ironically in view of their long history of conflict, the Vietnamese approach to warfare also drew heavily on Chinese models, especially the ideas developed by Mao Zedong during the Chinese civil war. Maoist doctrine emphasized the formation of a broad united front comprised of all elements of the population with the goal of national liberation, recognized the equal importance of political and military struggle, and relied on protracted war to exhaust stronger enemies.

Mao's classic *On Protracted War* set forth three stages of revolutionary warfare. In the first, essentially defensive stage, the revolutionary force was to withdraw, hide from the enemy, and mount sporadic hit-and-run attacks, the main goal being survival. During this phase, the focus was on revolutionary activity among the people to establish a secure base for future operations. Terrain was to be exchanged for time. Second came a stage of equilibrium, when caution began to give way to boldness and the defensive to the offensive. The guerrillas in this stage would extend their hold across the countryside and force the enemy to retreat into shrinking urban enclaves. Battles were larger, more frequent, and more conventional. The third and final stage of Maoist protracted warfare was the counteroffensive, when politics gave way to military operations and guerrilla warfare to full-scale conventional war.

The First Indochina War, 1946–1954

The three-decade struggle for Indochina began September 2, 1945, when the charismatic nationalist leader Ho Chi Minh declared the independence of Vietnam. The Vietnamese revolution was in many ways the personal

During World War II, Nguyen Ai Quoc changed his name to Ho Chi Minh ("he who enlightens") to conceal his communist background from his Chinese sponsors in the war against the Japanese. Beginning in spring 1945, Americans from the Office of Strategic Services served at Ho's headquarters in an effort to hasten the defeat of the Japanese.

creation of Ho Chi Minh. Born in the province of Nghe An, the cradle of Vietnamese revolutionaries, Ho settled in France and after World War I joined the French Communist Party. During the 1920s and 1930s, he served as a party functionary and revolutionary organizer in the Soviet Union, China, and Thailand. He returned to Vietnam in 1940 to found the Vietminh (League for the Independence of Vietnam) and organize yet another Vietnamese revolution against outside control. For a brief period after World War II, Ho attempted to negotiate a settlement with the colonial power, France, but the two sides could not agree on the most basic issues. In November 1946 mounting tensions sparked a war that in its various phases would last for nearly thirty years.

In their revolutionary war against France, the Vietnamese adapted Maoist doctrine to their own needs and conditions. Space was at a premium in Vietnam, and instead of trading terrain for time, as Mao had proposed, the Communist-led Vietminh rebels emphasized in the first stage organization and clandestine activity. From small cells of three to five people, they constructed "liberated areas." Avoiding pitched battles, they cultivated support among the people and where feasible ambushed exposed enemy forces. The Vietnamese also placed greater emphasis than Mao on external forces, increasingly relying on moral and material support from the Soviet Union and after 1949 from Mao's China. Perhaps even more important, public opinion in France was deemed crucial in influencing French policy, and the Vietnamese calculated that the longer the war lasted the more support would be generated for their cause. Given these factors, party theoretician Truong Chinh reasoned, absolute military superiority might not be necessary to launch the third and climactic phase of revolutionary war. To the Vietminh also, the third stage, although predominantly military, remained a civil war in which political struggle continued to be vital.

The Vietminh applied these ideas with some modification in the conflict against France. After the outbreak of war in late 1946, they melted into the countryside, concentrating on avoiding pitched battles, mobilizing the population into a united anti-French front, and harassing French forces. In January 1948, the Vietminh leadership announced the second stage of equilibrium warfare where they sought to regain the initiative, wear down enemy forces, and expand the territory under their control. The emphasis was still on guerrilla warfare, but larger units were created to mount mobile operations over large areas. The communist victory in China in 1949 significantly altered the character of the war in Vietnam, making available to the Vietminh material aid and protected sanctuaries. Thus buoyed, they prematurely shifted to the third phase in 1951, launching an offensive that proved disastrous. After three more years, in which they combined vigorous political activity in the countryside, guerrilla warfare, and conventional operations, the Vietminh mounted the climactic battle. General Vo Nguyen Giap pulled off a logistical miracle by moving vast numbers of men and quantities of supplies through mountainous terrain into a position to attack. Surrounding isolated French forces at the remote outpost of Dien Bien Phu in the northwestern corner of Vietnam, they gradually closed the ring and, while the world watched, decisively defeated a major European power.

The war won by the Vietminh at Dien Bien Phu was lost at the conference table in Geneva. Largely at the insistence of its allies, the Soviet Union and China, the Vietminh was compelled to accept a temporary partition of its country with national elections to be held in 1956. It took control of the area above the seventeenth parallel. In the south, however, a government headed by Ngo Dinh Diem and backed by the United States used the two-year interval to establish a separate South Vietnam, undermining the spirit if not the precise letter of the Geneva Accords. The Diem government ignored the call for elections in 1956. It also launched a ruthless and highly effective campaign to root out former Vietminh operatives who remained in the south.

Origins of the Second Indochina War

On the verge of extinction by 1957, the southern Vietminh launched a rebellion that would eventually grow into the Second Indochina War. Seeking merely to salvage what remained of the revolution of 1945, they mounted an armed struggle against the government, reactivating the intelligence and propaganda networks that had fallen into disuse after Geneva and initiating a vigorous campaign of political agitation in the villages. Largely as a result of Diem's oppressive policies, they found a receptive audience in the countryside—the peasants were like a "mound of straw ready to be ignited." The Vietminh attracted thousands of adherents and established a presence in numerous villages. The level of violence increased dramatically. In 1958, an estimated 700 government officials were assassinated; in 1960, 2,500. In

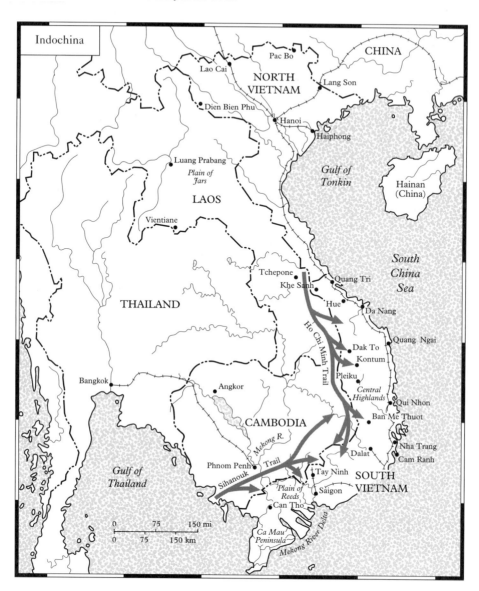

December 1960 the insurgents formed the National Liberation Front (NLF), a broad-based organization led by Communists but designed to rally all those disaffected with Diem by promising sweeping reforms and genuine independence.

North Vietnam gradually committed itself to the southern insurgency. In March 1957, Hanoi approved plans to modernize its own armed forces. Two years later, it formally authorized the resumption of armed struggle in the south and took measures to back it. The North Vietnamese established a special force to construct a supply route into the south—what would become the famed Ho Chi Minh Trail. They gradually increased the flow of men and matériel into the south and in September 1960 formally approved the shift to armed struggle.

From 1960 to 1965, the insurgency grew dramatically. Following the overthrow and assassination of Diem in a coup backed by the United States, South Vietnam degenerated into chaos, government succeeding government as through a revolving door. In December 1963, Hanoi instructed the NLF to step up its political agitation and military operations against the embattled South Vietnamese government. More important, it expanded infiltration into the south and even began to commit units of its own regular army. Over the next two years, the NLF extended its political control over the countryside, and its military units mounted increasingly bold attacks against South Vietnamese forces. The People's Army of North Vietnam (PAVN) was prepared for battle in the south. United States officials concluded by early 1965 that if they did not take drastic measures, South Vietnam would soon fall to the insurgents.

The NLF, PAVN, and Revolutionary War

To gain the upper hand in South Vietnam, NLF forces skillfully combined political and military "struggle." Their aims were to undermine the enemy's military and political positions and rally the people to their cause. In the political realm, NLF cadres created special organizations to give status to groups such as farmers, women, and youth. They used agitation and propaganda—"agitprop"—to arouse the people to the government's oppressiveness and lack of responsibility. They played to local grievances and used songs, skits, and speeches to explain their own program in terms the people could understand. Creating a mass organization where none had existed, they established a tightly knit political-military movement operating with often deadly efficiency from the village level to the central committee. By 1963, NLF strength in the rural areas of South Vietnam had grown to an estimated 300,000 people.

The NLF also assembled a highly disciplined and potent military organization. NLF main forces comprised some forty-seven battalions organized into five regiments and numbering by 1965 an estimated 80,000 of the "toughest, most experienced guerrilla fighters to be found anywhere in the world." Lightly equipped, usually clothed in the traditional black pajamas rather than uniforms, they relied on speed, surprise, and deception. Targets were chosen for maximum psychological significance, the NLF attacking villages and killing people who were deemed the greatest threats to their cause. They used violence selectively and judiciously to attain specified political ends—in general, to coerce or win over the population and undermine the legitimacy of the Saigon government. NLF units ambushed the forces of the South Vietnamese army (ARVN), attacked government-controlled hamlets, and sabotaged government communication links such as bridges, roads, and telephone or telegraph installations. They sought to provoke government officials to take oppressive measures that could be exploited politically. They assassinated and kidnapped village leaders who might cause problems for them, singling out those good officials whose removal could weaken the government and bad ones whose elimination could gain support for their cause.

The Main Forces were backed up by a popular army that operated at the village and hamlet level, a poorly equipped part-time guerrilla force of some 85,000 that worked the fields by day and ambushed and sabotaged by night.

By 1965, NLF forces were supported and in some areas supplanted by North Vietnamese regulars. Trained, organized, and equipped along Chinese lines, the People's Army of Vietnam numbered as many as 500,000 men and was supplemented by a ready reserve also of close to a half-million. Its divisions each possessed an authorized strength of 10,000 men, lightly armed and equipped for maximum mobility. Infantrymen generally carried Chinese-made pistols, 7.62-mm rifles, and three to five "potato-masher" grenades. Infantry divisions consisted of three infantry regiments when in the south, backed by weapons companies armed with 60-mm and 82-mm mortars, 57-mm and 75-mm recoilless rifles, and heavy machine guns. Training emphasized camouflage, the use of explosives, and small-unit tactics; field exercises were often conducted at night and under the most adverse conditions. The North Vietnamese made a virtue of the necessity of their light armament by constantly emphasizing that men, not weapons, constituted the decisive element in war. "People's war, not modern weapons and techniques, decides victory because war is the most acute form of struggle between man and man," party theorist Truong Chinh proclaimed in 1965.

The PAVN attempted to compensate for its weakness in firepower with rigorous discipline, tactical superiority, and careful preparation. As much as 50 percent of the training time of the PAVN soldier was spent in political education, and political commissars accompanied every unit above the company level. In battle, the North Vietnamese attempted to use the terrain to their best advantage, digging in even during rest periods and developing camouflage into a fine art. They tried to avoid battle except under favorable conditions and attacked the enemy at weak points rather than strong ones. They did not attempt to hold ground but rather sought to attack and withdraw before the enemy could react, hoping to inflict maximum casualties with rifles and automatic weapons in the opening moments of the fight. They were masters of the ambush. Actions of all sorts were planned and rehearsed with painstaking care. North Vietnamese units might take as much as a month to prepare the battlefield, massing ammunition and supplies, digging intricate systems of underground trenches, and stocking food and ammunition at attack points, ambush sites, and along withdrawal routes.

Mobility and small-unit maneuver were the hallmarks of North Vietnamese tactics. To minimize the impact of enemy firepower, PAVN forces attempted to close with the enemy as quickly as possible and to maintain close contact, even to the point of "hugging" and hand-to-hand combat. They preferred to overwhelm enemy forces by massing strength at a single point, and they excelled at encircling maneuvers with fifty to seventy-five men. Survival on the battlefield often depended on the ability to disengage, and North Vietnamese tactical doctrine held that the withdrawal was as important as the advance. At times, PAVN forces counterattacked to permit disengagement. If escape routes were blocked, they might attack a weak spot and slip away through the hole. Delaying forces were usually assigned the task of ambushing and harassing pursuers. Despite the lightness of its arma-

A detachment from the People's Army of Vietnam marches down a road as North Vietnamese civilians watch.

ments and a tendency to be repetitive and mechanistic in its tactical moves, the North Vietnamese army was a formidable fighting force. The French-born combat historian Bernard Fall did not exaggerate when he described it in September 1965 as "one of the best infantry combat forces in the world, capable of incredible feats of endurance and raw courage even against vastly superior firepower and under the worst physical conditions."

The United States: Counterinsurgency and Limited War

By the mid-1960s, Vietnam had become a focal point of United States' foreign policy. Perceiving the Soviet Union as a mortal threat, the Truman administration, in the aftermath of World War II, had committed itself to the containment of communist expansion. From the outbreak of revolution in Vietnam, U.S. policy makers had viewed Ho Chi Minh's Vietminh as an instrument of Moscow's larger global designs. Thus in early 1950, the United States began to provide military and economic aid to the French to assist in the suppression of the Vietminh insurgency. By 1954, Washington was paying nearly 80 percent of the cost of the war. When the French were defeated, the United States filled the vacuum, assisting the Diem government to solidify its position and providing lavish aid to sustain in South

Vietnam an independent, non-communist government that could stand as a bulwark against further communist expansion in Southeast Asia.

In the 1960s, Vietnam became a test case for new U.S. counterinsurgency doctrines. The Eisenhower administration had responded to the outbreak of war in Vietnam by providing the Diem government additional aid and U.S. military advisers. The Kennedy administration went further. Kennedy and his advisers were persuaded that so-called "brush-fire" wars such as the one taking place in Vietnam represented the new Soviet strategy for world domination. By fighting at a low level in peripheral areas, the communist adversary could avoid a nuclear confrontation and chip away at free-world strength. Kennedy and his advisers therefore scrapped Eisenhower's New Look defense policy, which had emphasized nuclear weapons and Massive Retaliation, and adopted a strategy of "Flexible Response" that permitted different types of military moves at different levels. They launched in 1961 a massive buildup of conventional forces to balance America's nuclear arsenal and implement Flexible Response.

The Kennedy administration also placed great emphasis on counterinsurgency. The president himself took a keen interest in the subject, and the works of Mao Zedong became required reading for top U.S. officials. Kennedy gave his blessings to the U.S. Army's elite Green Berets and required all the military services to develop counterinsurgency doctrine.

The administration first applied its new ideas and methods in Vietnam. As a senator, Kennedy had once referred to Vietnam as the "cornerstone of the free world in Southeast Asia." He and his advisers increasingly viewed it as a test case of America's determination to uphold its commitments and its capacity to meet the challenges of guerrilla warfare in the emerging nations. Between 1961 and 1963, the president thus launched a full-scale counterinsurgency program in Vietnam, approving a massive increase in U.S. military and economic aid and enlarging the number of U.S. advisers to more than 16,000.

The Kennedy program attacked the NLF insurgency on several fronts. Militarily, the United States provided the South Vietnamese army the latest hardware including armored personnel carriers, helicopters, and aircraft. Buoyed by American aid and advisers, the South Vietnamese armed forces took the offensive against the guerrillas. U.S. advisers performed ever-widening tasks. Special Forces units conducted civic action programs among the primitive peoples of the Central Highlands. Helicopter pilots dropped detachments of South Vietnamese troops into battle zones deep in the swamps and picked up the dead and wounded. Americans went with Vietnamese trainees on bombing and strafing missions and, when the Vietnamese ran short of pilots, flew the planes themselves. Army officers and enlisted men conducted expanded training programs for the South Vietnamese army, and advisers down to the battalion level accompanied its units on combat missions.

U.S. military and civilian advisers also assisted the South Vietnamese government in implementing the so-called Strategic Hamlet program. Developed by the British counterinsurgency expert Sir Robert Thompson on the basis of experiences in Malaya, the program was designed to isolate the

NLF from the people of South Vietnam. Peasants from scattered villages were brought together into hamlets surrounded by moats and bamboo stake fences and defended by military forces. The hamlets were intended to protect the people against the guerrillas and also to serve as an instrument for a social and economic revolution to draw the people to the government. Village elections, land reform, and the establishment of schools and medical services were to persuade the people that life under the South Vietnamese government offered more than the NLF. The objective, U.S. counterinsurgency expert Roger Hilsman observed, was to reduce the guerrillas to "hungry, marauding bands of outlaws devoting all their energies to remaining alive," forcing them out into the open where they would have to fight the South Vietnamese army on its terms.

The Kennedy counterinsurgency program failed. The Strategic Hamlet program was flawed both in conception and execution. It had worked well in Malaya, where Malay villages were fortified against Chinese insurgents, but in Vietnam the hamlets were to be erected against Vietnamese, many of whom had lived among the villagers for years, and they were easily infiltrated. In some regions, the hamlets could not be established without massive uprooting of the peasantry, and the displacement of people from ancestral lands added to the discontent that already pervaded the countryside. In many cases, the government moved too far too fast in implementing the program, establishing hamlets in areas where no real security existed. The vulnerable settlements were thus quickly overrun or infiltrated by the insurgents. Many of the hamlets lacked adequate defenses. Some were spread over such a large area that it would have required a full division to defend them. In the hands of Diem and his sinister brother-in-law, Ngo Dinh Nhu, moreover, the program alienated the people rather than attracted them to the government.

Militarily, the Kennedy program also failed. Despite relentless pressure from the White House, the armed services refused to embrace counterinsurgency and insisted on fighting the war the way they knew how. Even with modern aircraft, it proved impossible to locate the guerrillas amidst the dense forests and swampy paddy lands. The very nature of U.S.–South Vietnamese operations, an air strike followed by the landing of troops, gave the insurgents warning and permitted them to slip away. ARVN forces would often bomb and strafe large areas and land sizable detachments of troops with little result, and when they withdrew the guerrillas simply reoccupied the region. The insurgents learned how to bring down slow, clumsy helicopters with small arms. Sometimes they would lie in hiding until the helicopters had departed and then ambush the landing force. As operations became more costly, ARVN commanders, apparently under orders from Diem, relied more and more on air power and refused to risk their troops in battle.

The Battle of Ap Bac, 1963

The shift in the fortunes of war was dramatically revealed in January 1963. An American adviser, the legendary Colonel John Paul Vann, pressed his

South Vietnamese division commander to attack three guerrilla companies near the village of Ap Bac. The South Vietnamese commander delayed for a day, giving the NLF time to learn of the operation and prepare deadly defenses. Outnumbering the enemy ten to one—the classic ratio for success against guerrillas—the South Vietnamese planned a three-pronged assault. At the first signs of resistance, however, the attacking forces balked. One prong simply refused to attack. Other units failed to block enemy escape routes. The battle ended ingloriously with the South Vietnamese firing on each other while the enemy slipped away. The vastly superior ARVN forces suffered sixty-one dead and one hundred wounded, while the NLF left only three bodies behind. Continuing to think in conventional warfare terms, the U.S. command in Saigon claimed victory because the enemy had abandoned its territory. Those in the field and the American reporters who covered the action knew better.

By 1965, the United States faced a major turning point in Vietnam. Following the overthrow and assassination of Diem and the instability that followed, the NLF insurgency had gained momentum. Supported by a steadily growing flow of men and supplies from North Vietnam, the insurgents took advantage of the near anarchy in the south. By early 1965, the NLF had secured uncontested control of the vital Mekong Delta region south of Saigon and appeared capable of splitting the country in half. The corruption-ridden South Vietnamese army, even with sharply increased U.S. aid, could not slow, much less stop, the enemy onslaught.

The administration of Lyndon Baines Johnson saw little choice but to escalate the U.S. commitment. Responding to the urgent warnings of his advisers that South Vietnam was on the verge of collapse, the president in February 1965 mounted regular, sustained bombing raids against North Vietnam. The bombing had only a marginal impact on the war, however, and by late spring General William Westmoreland, head of the U.S. military assistance program in Vietnam, requested a massive increase in American military forces and the commitment of U.S. combat units to reverse a rapidly deteriorating situation. After several weeks of intensive deliberations, the president in late July made what amounted to a decision for full-scale war in Vietnam, committing himself to provide U.S. combat support as needed.

Limited War in Theory and Practice

Responding to the challenge in Vietnam, Johnson and his advisers were deeply influenced by the limited war theory so much in vogue in the United States during the 1950s and 1960s. When the Soviet Union developed effective delivery systems for nuclear weapons, it was obvious to many military theorists that the Eisenhower administration's emphasis on Massive Retaliation could not work. With nothing but nuclear weapons as a deterrent, the United States in responding to communist challenges in peripheral areas would face the unthinkable choice of starting a nuclear war or doing nothing.

To escape that dilemma and find the means to contain communist expansion without risking a nuclear holocaust, civilian and military theorists advocated the alternative of limited war. Such a strategy would harness the nation's military power more closely to the attainment of its political objectives. Through Flexible Response, a variety of military instruments would be readied to respond to different types of threats at different levels. The amount of force to be employed in any situation would be limited to that necessary to achieve the political aim. The objective was not to destroy an opponent but to persuade him to break off the conflict short of achieving his goals and without resorting to nuclear war.

The limited-war theorists provided a set of broad guidelines for the conduct of that sort of conflict. Statesmen must "scrupulously limit" the political objectives and clearly communicate them to the enemy. They must make every effort to keep open diplomatic channels to terminate the war through negotiations on the basis of limited objectives. They must keep the war precisely limited in terms of geography and must restrict the force used to that amount necessary to attain the political objectives. Limited war must be directed by the civilian leadership. The special needs of the military should not affect its conduct, and indeed the military must be a controllable instrument of national policy.

Limited-war theory also set forth methods for using military power to persuade an adversary to act in the desired way. Military action was less important for the damage it did, according to this reasoning, than for the message it sent. War became a sort of bargaining process through which force was employed to persuade an enemy that persisting in what he was doing would be too expensive to continue. "The object," political scientist Thomas Schelling observed, "is to exact good behavior or to oblige discontinuance of mischief, not to destroy the subject altogether." The implicit assumption was that the use of force could be orchestrated in such a way as to communicate precise and specific signals and that an opponent would back down in the face of such threats or pressure.

Limited-war theory had numerous flaws. It was primarily an academic, rather than a military concept, and it drastically misunderstood the dynamics of war. Its authors seemed to say that since limited war was mainly about bargaining and diplomacy, it required no knowledge of military matters and indeed military considerations should not affect its conduct. Despite the popular frustrations caused by fighting a limited war in Korea, the theorists seemed grandly indifferent to the domestic political problems it posed. Political scientist Robert Osgood conceded that this type of conflict ran counter to the American way of war and that Americans might not easily accept the "galling but indispensable restraints" required by it. But he neatly dodged the problem with platitudes, calling for candor and courage on the part of leaders and surmising that if Americans were treated as adults they would respond accordingly. Limited-war theorists also devoted more effort to explaining why this type of war should be fought rather than how it was to be fought. In terms of bargaining theory, moreover, they assumed a greater capacity than was warranted on the part of a gigantic bureaucracy like the United States government to send clear, precise signals, and they reduced the behavior of potential enemies to that of laboratory rats. These problems, however, are more obvious in retrospect than they were at the time.

The Johnson administration's strategy in Vietnam was deeply influenced by limited-war theory. Fearful that the actions they were taking to prevent a third world war might themselves provoke a dangerous confrontation with the Soviet Union and China, the president and his top civilian advisers put precise geographical limits on the war. They kept their military commanders on a tight rein, rejecting proposals to invade enemy sanctuaries in Laos, Cambodia, and North Vietnam, mine Haiphong Harbor, and bomb near the Chinese border. Vividly recalling the Korean War and the bitter controversy between President Harry S Truman and General Douglas MacArthur, Johnson and his civilian advisers fretted about military recklessness and a MacArthur-like challenge to civilian authority. "General, I have a lot riding on you," the president told Westmoreland in February 1966. "I hope you don't pull a MacArthur on me."

The administration fought the war according to the political dictates of limited-war theory. The theory of gradual escalation presumed that a steady increase in the level of military pressure would coerce an adversary into compliance. Thus the United States slowly increased the bombing and steadily expanded the number of U.S. troops and the intensity of ground operations. At no point did the president accede to the full requests of his military commanders. Yet once underway, the process of escalation achieved a momentum of its own, the failure of one level of force providing justification for the next level. By 1967, the United States had concentrated in Vietnam close to 500,000 men, roughly one-half its tactical airpower, and 30 percent of its naval strength. It was spending more than 2 billion dollars per month on the war.

A Modern, High-Tech Military Machine

The forces the United States sent to Vietnam were the best that money and modern technology could provide. During the Kennedy years, Secretary of Defense Robert S. McNamara had presided over a dramatic expansion and reorganization of the U.S. military to meet the perceived threats of a direct Soviet attack on Western Europe, limited conventional wars like Korea, and "brush-fire" wars in the Third World.

Although Vietnam was primarily a land war, air and sea power played an important role. Refitted World War II battleships pounded North Vietnamese bases from offshore. Conventional and nuclear-powered aircraft carriers were deployed in the Gulf of Tonkin, and their aircraft conducted Operation "Rolling Thunder" against North Vietnam from March 1965 until October 1968. Air force F-105 Thunderchiefs (known as "Thuds" by their pilots) carrying 7,500 pounds of bombs were also workhorses in the air war against North Vietnam. Air force and navy aircraft bombed enemy supply lines and staging areas in North and South Vietnam and flew close air-support missions for American and South Vietnamese forces in the field. The most formidable weapon—and most feared by the enemy—was the giant B-52 bomber that flew at 30,000 feet, carried a payload of 58,000 pounds, and left enormous craters in its path of destruction.

In what Westmoreland described as "the most sophisticated war in history," the United States attempted to exploit its technological superiority to cope with the peculiar problems posed by a guerrilla war. To locate an ever-elusive enemy, the military used small portable radar units and "people sniffers," which picked up the odor of human urine. IBM 1430 computers were programmed to predict likely times and places of enemy attacks. Herbicides were used on a wide scale and with devastating ecological and human consequences to deprive the NLF of natural cover. C-47 transports were converted into awesome gunships called "Puff the Magic Dragon" that could fire 18,000 rounds per minute.

The army that fought in Vietnam was one of the best clothed, best equipped, and best prepared the nation had ever sent to war. McNamara had increased the strength of the army to nearly one million men, raised the number of combat-ready divisions from eleven to sixteen, vastly expanded airlift capacity, and stockpiled huge quantities of equipment. The army was reorganized to create a flexible, adaptable organization capable of meeting its varied missions.

Innovations in equipment drastically increased its mobility and firepower. The advent of armored personnel carriers and troop-carrying helicopters significantly altered the nature of infantry operations. Helmets, pistols, and mortars were similar to those used in Korea, and machine guns and artillery were improved versions of weapons long in use, but two new

U.S. soldiers dismounting from a helicopter in a search and destroy operation. Airborne insertions often occurred when intelligence reported the presence of enemy soldiers. If the landing unit made contact with enemy forces, additional units "piled on" in an attempt to surround and destroy the enemy.

weapons vastly increased the firepower of the individual infantryman. The M-79 grenade launcher permitted the use of grenades at ranges up to 350 meters with far greater accuracy and were particularly useful in ambushes and against machine-gun nests. Claymore mines, which weighed only 3.5 pounds, were easy to place, had a destructive area of up to fifty meters, and were valuable in ambushes.

A major innovation of the 1960s was the creation of an air-cavalry division by the U.S. Army. Helicopters had been used effectively in restricted roles in Korea, and as their technology improved their potential began to seem almost limitless. They were widely employed during the advisory years in Vietnam and seemed increasingly to provide the solution to the difficult problem of locating and engaging elusive guerrillas in difficult terrain. After a period of tests, McNamara activated the 1st Cavalry Division (Airmobile) in June 1965. The new division made large-scale airmobile operations possible. Although lightly armed, it compensated with its fast-strike capability; its helicopters could land as many as 10,000 troops in battle zones within hours. Its greatest assets were its ability to cover all types of terrain, maneuver over large areas, react quickly to enemy attacks and reinforce embattled units, and conduct raids behind enemy lines. Thus by July 1965, two nations with very different military traditions and two powerful and quite different military forces were set to engage each other in Vietnam.

Escalation and Stalemate, 1965–1968

By the time the United States escalated the war in 1965, North Vietnam and the NLF appeared on the verge of victory. Sensing in the growing chaos in South Vietnam a splendid opportunity to attain long-sought goals, Hanoi had sharply escalated the war. North Vietnamese leaders still thought in terms of Maoist doctrine, a protracted struggle with victory to be attained through a series of stages. Always flexible in their thinking, however, their new strategy called for a gradual shift from low-level action to the use of large-scale military forces to annihilate enemy main forces. The final stage would be a military offensive in the rural areas and a popular uprising in the cities that would leave the United States no choice but to pull out of South Vietnam. In 1964 and 1965, the North Vietnamese implemented their strategy with great success. PAVN and NLF main forces gradually extended their control over the strategic Central Highlands of South Vietnam while NLF guerrillas scored equally impressive gains in the Mekong Delta south of Saigon. By early 1965, the insurgents controlled half the population and more than half the territory of South Vietnam. The only secure areas were the major cities, and they were increasingly threatened by civil disturbances.

In escalating the war, the Johnson administration sought to head off what seemed a certain enemy victory and to preserve an independent, non-communist South Vietnam. The administration's strategy was based on the assumption that if the United States slowly increased the level of military pain, it would reach a point at which the North Vietnamese would decide that the costs were greater than the potential gain. The Rolling Thunder bombing program initiated in March 1965 and gradually expanded thereafter was designed to reduce the infiltration of men and supplies into South Vietnam and to pressure North Vietnam into stopping its support of the insurgency. With the increased ground forces provided him in July 1965, General Westmoreland sought first to stem the momentum of communist advances in the countryside and to provide security in the urban areas. This accomplished, he planned to launch a number of major search-and-destroy operations to cripple enemy main-force units and break the NLF hold on the countryside. Once the enemy's regular forces had been destroyed, he reasoned, the South Vietnamese government would be able to stabilize its position and "pacify" the countryside, and the enemy would have no choice but to negotiate on terms acceptable to the United States. The marines were given responsibility for operations in the northern provinces (I Corps), while the army was assigned the task in the Central Highlands, along the central coast, and in the region around Saigon. In the meantime, the ARVN, with the support of U.S. civilian and military advisers, was to launch a "pacification" program to break the NLF hold on the countryside and build support for South Vietnam's government.

Battle of the Ia Drang, 1965

The first major clash of opposing armies came in the Ia Drang valley in the Central Highlands in late 1965. As part of its winter-spring campaign of 1965–1966, Hanoi ordered a PAVN army corps to execute a series of operations around Pleiku in the Central Highlands with the object of striking a knockout blow. The first stage of the operation was an attack on a U.S. Special Forces camp near Plei Me near the Cambodian border. Using a classic lure-and-ambush tactic, the North Vietnamese followed with the real object of their plan, a major attack against the South Vietnamese relief column sent to save the base. Using ground forces, artillery, and especially tactical air support and relying—as they would throughout the war—on the superiority of their firepower, the United States and South Vietnam launched a furious counterattack on the forces besieging Plei Me and repulsed the North Vietnamese ambush of the relief column. Their plan frustrated, the PAVN forces slipped away to their base areas in Cambodia. According to U.S. estimates, in this first encounter, the North Vietnamese lost as many as 850 killed and 1,700 wounded.

Seeking to follow up this initial success, Westmoreland dispatched the 1st Cavalry Division on search-and-destroy operations against retreating enemy forces. From October 28 to November 14, U.S. forces conducted a series of air and ground searches in the Ia Drang valley punctuated by sporadic and violent clashes. The largest action occurred on November 14 when four American companies fell upon a North Vietnamese regiment at

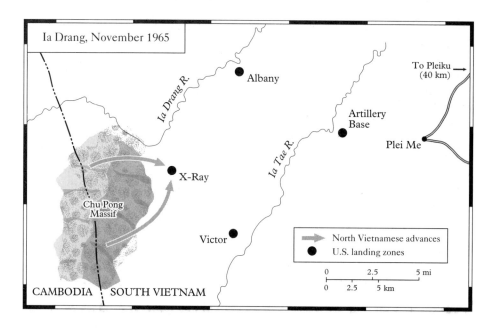

Ia Drang, November 1965

landing zone X-Ray. As at Plei Me, U.S. firepower eventually saved the day, artillery from nearby landing zones pouring more than 8,000 rounds against enemy positions, and air force fighter-bombers and even giant B-52s from Guam flying close air support. Pounded relentlessly for nearly two days, the battered North Vietnamese eventually withdrew to their sanctuaries. The following day, an American battalion stumbled into a disastrous ambush at nearby landing zone Albany, suffering huge casualties. In all, the North Vietnamese lost an estimated 3,000 killed in the Ia Drang fighting, the United States 300.

It remains difficult even today to assess this first (and one of the few) major battles of the Vietnam War. Thinking in entirely conventional terms, the U.S. military claimed victory because of the heavy losses it inflicted and because the enemy had been forced to withdraw from the battlefield. Some commentators also hailed as unusual if not indeed unique among America's first battles the outstanding performance of U.S. troops in this, their "blooding." North Vietnam indeed suffered staggering losses. In the aftermath of the Ia Drang, Giap reverted to guerrilla warfare and made major tactical adjustments to better cope with U.S. firepower. Still, U.S. officials were also stunned by the severity of their losses and abandoned any hope that success could be achieved at light cost. Americans failed to recognize, moreover, that in this kind of warfare if the enemy did not lose, it won. Finding in the Ia Drang confirmation of his belief that a search-and-destroy strategy would break the enemy's will to fight, Westmoreland made no major adjustments in his approach to the war. The Ia Drang battle thus set the tone for much of what lay ahead: more and larger search-and-destroy missions, numerous "victories"—and ultimately frustration.

Throughout 1966 and 1967, the United States continued to escalate the war. Rolling Thunder bombing sorties increased from 25,000 in 1965 to

U.S. Air Force F-5 Freedom Fighter engaged in close air support. Ground troops particularly valued missions against enemy bunkers and fortified positions. Air attacks proved less successful, however, in interdicting supplies from North Vietnam.

108,000 in 1967, and the tonnage of bombs dropped increased from 63,000 to 226,000. The number of ground troops grew from 184,300 at the end of 1965 to 485,600 at the end of 1967. Furnished with thousands of new ground troops and a massive arsenal of modern weaponry, Westmoreland took the war to the enemy. Throughout 1966 and 1967, intensive fighting raged across much of South Vietnam. Along the demilitarized zone, marines and North Vietnamese regulars were dug in like the armies of World War I, pounding each other relentlessly with artillery. In the jungle areas, small American units probed for a hidden enemy in a manner comparable to the Pacific island campaigns of World War II.

Increasingly, however, Westmoreland concentrated on large-scale search-and-destroy missions against enemy base areas. Operation Cedar Falls, a major campaign of early 1967, sent some 30,000 U.S. troops against the Iron Triangle, an NLF stronghold just north of Saigon. After B-52s saturated the area with bombs, U.S. troops surrounded it, and helicopters dropped large numbers of specially trained combat forces into the villages. Following removal of the population, giant Rome plows with huge spikes on the front leveled the area, destroying what remained of the vegetation and leaving the guerrillas no place to hide. The region was then burned and bombed again to destroy the miles of underground tunnels that formed the enemy military complex.

The most that could be achieved was a stalemate. North Vietnam was stunned by American intervention in 1965 and alarmed by the effectiveness of U.S. firepower in the Ia Drang. Hanoi thus abandoned any hope of an early victory and settled in for a protracted struggle against a greatly strengthened enemy. Learning from their war against France, the North Vietnamese leadership increasingly counted on the weakness of the South Vietnamese regime and antiwar opposition in the United States. The key to exploiting these advantages, they reasoned, was to keep maximum military pressure on the enemy without needlessly exposing their own forces to destruction. PAVN and NLF units thus retreated to their sanctuaries, seeking to avoid U.S. search-and-destroy operations. At the same time, they constantly harassed exposed U.S. and ARVN troops and launched attacks of up to regimental size at times and places of their own choosing. Hanoi's strategists concentrated against the South Vietnamese government and army to exploit their weaknesses and ultimately force their collapse. To keep the American casualty lists as high as possible and thereby keep the war on the front pages in the United States, they also attacked U.S. forces. They used tactics of "clinging to the G.I.s' belts" to minimize the effectiveness of U.S. artillery and air support. High priority was still given to political agitation, especially in the cities of South Vietnam that were swollen with increasing numbers of restless and disaffected refugees.

North Vietnam effectively countered the U.S. air war. By 1967, the tonnage of bombs dropped on North Vietnam exceeded that dropped on Germany, Italy, and Japan during World War II. America's heavy reliance on air power seriously underestimated the commitment of the North Vietnamese and overestimated the capabilities of strategic bombing. The gradual escalation of the bombing permitted the North Vietnamese to protect vital resources, and losses were more than made up by expanded aid from China and the Soviet Union. The North Vietnamese showed a remarkable capacity for coping with the bombing, repairing bridges and railroads within hours after destruction. The daily pounding from the air seemed to stiffen their will, and they showed no sign of bending under the pressure. The rate of infiltration into the south increased after the bombing was started and continued to increase as it expanded. By late 1967, North Vietnamese forces were four times greater than in 1965.

The North Vietnamese also blunted U.S. operations on the ground. Westmoreland's strategy of attrition assumed that the United States could inflict intolerable losses while keeping its own losses within acceptable bounds, an assumption that flew in the face of past experience with land wars on the Asian continent and the realities in Vietnam. An estimated 200,000 North Vietnamese came of draft age each year, and Hanoi was able to match each American escalation. Moreover, the conditions under which the war was fought permitted North Vietnam to control its losses. The North Vietnamese and NLF were generally able to avoid contact when it suited them. They fought at times and places of their own choosing and on ground favorable to them. If losses reached unacceptable proportions, they melted into the jungles or retreated into sanctuaries in North Vietnam, Laos, or Cambodia. North Vietnamese and NLF forces were hurt, sometimes badly, but their main forces could not be destroyed. They retained the strategic initiative and could strike sharply when and where they chose. Westmoreland did not have sufficient forces to wage war against enemy regulars and control the countryside. The NLF political structure thus remained intact, and even in areas such as the Iron Triangle, when American forces moved on to fight elsewhere, the NLF quietly slipped back in. It all added up to a "state of irresolution," journalist Robert Shaplen observed in 1967.

With the military situation a stalemate, the political aspect assumed greater importance, and the fundamental problem, the Saigon government, remained unresolved. A coalition of generals headed by Nguyen Cao Ky and Nguyen Van Thieu finally emerged from the long series of coups and countercoups from 1963 to 1965, but it represented none of the multiplicity of political factions in the south. Neither the government nor the United States was capable of broadening South Vietnam's narrow political base. The huge influx of Americans after 1965 and expansion of the war created problems that even the most responsible and effective government would have found difficult to handle. The massive bombing and artillery fire drove thousands of sullen refugees into already overcrowded cities. The South Vietnamese economy was geared around providing services to the Americans and quickly reached the point where it could not absorb the ever-expanding volume of money and goods. In the cities, corruption, profiteering, and vice ran rampant.

As the war dragged on inconclusively, moreover, popular support in the United States began to erode, and by the end of 1967 the American

In April 1967, General William C. Westmoreland briefed President Johnson and his top advisors on the need to send additional troops to Vietnam. By approving an increase of 50,000 instead of 200,000, the president refused to expand the war dramatically, but he also refused to accept Robert S. McNamara's advice about making basic changes in policy toward Vietnam.

people had become polarized over Vietnam as no other issue since their own Civil War a century earlier. Those labeled "hawks" protested the restraints imposed on the military and demanded that Johnson do what was necessary to win or get out of Vietnam. At the other extreme, growing numbers of so-called "doves" protested that the war was immoral or unnecessary or both and demanded that the United States get out of Vietnam. At this point in the war, the great majority of Americans rejected both extremes, but as the war dragged on and the debate became more divisive, disillusionment increased markedly. Public support for the war dropped sharply in 1967, and Johnson's approval rating fell even further, dipping to a low 28 percent in October.

The Tet Offensive, 1968

In the spring and summer of 1967, the North Vietnamese decided to attempt to break an increasingly costly deadlock. To lure American troops away from the major population centers and maintain high U.S. casualties, a series of large-scale diversionary attacks was to be launched in remote areas. These would be followed by coordinated NLF assaults against the major cities and towns of South Vietnam designed to weaken the government and ignite a "general uprising" among the people. At the same time efforts would be made to open negotiations with the United States. Hanoi probably hoped through these coordinated actions to get the bombing stopped, weaken the Saigon regime, exacerbate differences between the United States and its South Vietnamese ally, and intensify pressures for a change in U.S. policy. Its ultimate objective was to secure an acceptable settlement, the minimum ingredients of which would be a coalition government and U.S. withdrawal.

    The first phase of the North Vietnamese plan worked to perfection. In October and November, PAVN forces attacked the Marine base at Con Thien across the Laotian border and the towns of Loc Ninh and Song Be near Saigon and Dak To in the Central Highlands. Shortly after, two PAVN divisions laid siege to the Marine garrison at Khe Sanh near the Laotian border. Westmoreland quickly dispatched reinforcements to these embattled areas, in each case driving back the enemy and inflicting heavy losses, but in the process dispersing his forces and leaving the cities vulnerable. By the end of the year, moreover, the attention of Westmoreland, President Johnson, and indeed much of the nation was riveted on Khe Sanh, which many Americans assumed was General Giap's play for a repetition of his smashing victory at Dien Bien Phu.

    During the Tet holiday of early 1968, the North Vietnamese and NLF launched the second and major phase of their offensive. On January 30, 1968, the NLF carried out a series of attacks extending across the length of the country. In all, they struck thirty-six of forty-four provincial capitals, five of the six major cities, sixty-four district capitals, and fifty hamlets. In Saigon, they mounted a daring raid on the U.S. embassy, briefly penetrating

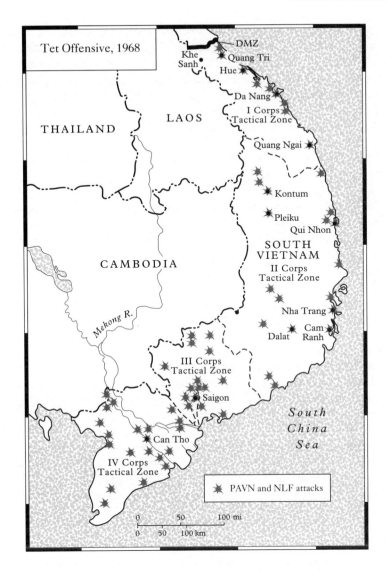

Tet Offensive, 1968

DMZ
Khe Sanh
Quang Tri
Hue
Da Nang
I Corps Tactical Zone
THAILAND
LAOS
Quang Ngai
Kontum
Pleiku
Qui Nhon
SOUTH VIETNAM
II Corps Tactical Zone
CAMBODIA
Mekong R.
Nha Trang
Dalat   Cam Ranh
III Corps Tactical Zone
Saigon
South China Sea
Can Tho
IV Corps Tactical Zone

* PAVN and NLF attacks

0   50   100 mi
0   50   100 km

the compound, and assaulted Tan Son Nhut airport, the presidential palace, and the headquarters of South Vietnam's general staff. In Hue, 7,500 NLF and PAVN troops stormed and eventually took control of the ancient Citadel, the interior town that had been the seat of the emperors of the ancient kingdom of Vietnam.

Although taken by surprise, the United States and South Vietnam recovered quickly. The initial attacks were poorly coordinated, and premature assaults in some areas enabled Westmoreland to get reinforcements to vulnerable spots. In addition, the attackers were slow to capitalize on their early successes, giving the U.S. and South Vietnam time to mount strong defenses. In Saigon, U.S. and ARVN forces held off the initial attack and within several days had cleared the city, inflicting huge casualties, taking large numbers of prisoners, and forcing the remnants to melt into the countryside. Elsewhere, the result was much the same. ARVN fought better under pressure than anyone could have anticipated, and the United States and South Vietnam used their superior mobility and firepower to devastating advantage. The NLF launched a second round of attacks on February 18, but these were confined largely to rocket and mortar barrages against military installations and had little effect.

The Battle for Hue

Hue was the major exception. The battle to liberate that city pitted two PAVN regiments and two NLF battalions against eight U.S. and thirteen ARVN battalions, lasted from January 31 to March 2, and was one of the most savage and destructive battles of the entire war. For those ARVN forces and U.S. Marines who participated, the struggle for Hue involved some of the most brutal and deadly fighting since World War II.

Recognizing the value of holding even temporarily the cultural and religious center of the nation, North Vietnamese and NLF forces had infiltrated Hue before Tet, carefully stockpiling weapons and ammunition. They attained near-complete surprise, and as advance units took key points, reinforcements poured into the city. Undermanned because of holiday furloughs, ARVN responded ineffectually. Within hours of the opening of the battle, North Vietnamese and NLF units controlled all of the Citadel and much of the city south of the Perfume River, even threatening the headquarters of the U.S. military command.

Initial U.S. and South Vietnamese efforts to retake the city failed. ARVN units dispatched to liberate Hue were battered by carefully planned enemy ambushes. United States and ARVN forces staged a major attack on February 1, but met fierce resistance from well-emplaced enemy forces. They made painfully slow progress, only to be hurled back on February 6 by a PAVN/NLF counterattack.

Eventually, massive force and heavy fighting were needed to retake the city. At first reluctant to destroy Hue's architectural treasures, the United States and South Vietnam in time bowed to expediency. Ships from the U.S. Seventh Fleet, aircraft, and artillery pounded enemy positions, and tanks and flamethrowers cleared the way for attacking forces. Both sides used tear gas, and Hue was the only battle of the war where gas masks were regularly worn. Backed by massive firepower, South Vietnamese and U.S. forces launched a full-scale attack on February 9 against dug-in enemy forces and well-concealed snipers. The enemy responded the following day, counterattacking and decimating an entire ARVN battalion. Slowly, U.S. and South Vietnamese forces clawed their way, house by house, into the city, reaching the moat of the Citadel by February 21. After a night of bitter, hand-to-hand combat, advance ARVN units raised the South Vietnamese flag over the Citadel. That same day, another South Vietnamese unit retook the Imperial Palace. After more than a week of mopping up operations, Hue was finally liberated on March 2.

It remains difficult twenty-five years after the event to assess the impact of the battles of Tet. The North Vietnamese and NLF did not force the collapse of South Vietnam. They were unable to establish any firm positions in the urban areas, and the South Vietnamese people did not rise up to welcome them as "liberators." NLF and PAVN battle deaths have been estimated as high as 40,000, and although this figure may be inflated, the losses were huge. The NLF bore the brunt of the fighting throughout South Vietnam. Its main force units were decimated and would never completely recover, and its political infrastructure suffered crippling losses.

If in these terms Tet represented a defeat for North Vietnam and the NLF, it was still a costly and in some ways hollow victory for the United States and South Vietnam. ARVN forces had to be withdrawn from the countryside to defend the cities, and the pacification program incurred another major setback. The destruction visited upon the cities heaped formidable new problems on a government that had shown only limited capacity to deal with the routine. American and South Vietnamese losses did not approach those of the enemy, but they were still high: in the first two weeks of the Tet campaigns, the United States lost 1,100 killed in action and South Vietnam 2,300. An estimated 12,500 civilians were killed, and Tet created as many as one million new refugees. In Hue during the period of PAVN/NLF "liberation," 2,800 civilians were massacred and buried in mass graves. As with so much of the war, there was a great deal of destruction and suffering, but no clear-cut winner or loser.

Perhaps the major impact of Tet was in the United States. Westmoreland insisted that the attacks had been repulsed and that there was no need to fear a major setback, and administration officials publicly echoed his statements. Johnson and his advisers were shocked by the suddenness and magnitude of the offensive, however, and intelligence estimates were much more pessimistic than Westmoreland. Among the general public, Tet caused a mood of gloom. For those who had long opposed the conflict and some who had supported it, Tet seemed to provide compelling evidence of its folly. "The war in Vietnam is unwinnable," the columnist Joseph Kraft concluded, "and the longer it goes on the more the Americans . . . will be subjected to losses and humiliation." Approval of Johnson's handling of the war, which had risen significantly in late 1967, again plummeted sharply in 1968, hitting an all-time low of 26 percent during Tet. Senator Eugene McCarthy's strong showing against the president in the New Hampshire primary suggested the political damage done by the war. Johnson was further threatened by Senator Robert Kennedy's announcement that he too would run on an antiwar platform.

Tet eventually forced Johnson to approve important changes of policy. After nearly two months of soul-searching and intensive internal debate, the president rejected his military advisers' proposals for a major escalation of the war. In a dramatic speech on March 31, 1968, he went still further, cutting back the bombing to the area just north of the demilitarized zone, making clear his willingness to negotiate, and, to underscore his seriousness, withdrawing from the presidential race.

Johnson's speech is usually cited as a major turning point in the war, and in some ways it was. It brought an end to the policy of gradual escalation, yet it did not represent a change of goals. Apparent U.S. success in the battles of Tet reinforced the conviction of the president and some of his advisers that they could yet secure an independent, non-communist South Vietnam. By rejecting major troop reinforcements, reducing the bombing, shifting some of the fighting to the South Vietnamese, and withdrawing from the presidential race, Johnson hoped to salvage his policy at least to the end of his term. The president's March 31 speech did not represent a change of objective as much as a shift of tactics to sustain a policy that had come under bitter attack.

For the North Vietnamese and NLF as well, Tet produced disillusionment, even despair. The failure of the offensive to attain its major goals and the heavy losses suffered appear to have provoked heated internal debate. The Vietnamese recognized, as one document put it, that "Victory will come to us, not suddenly, but in a complicated and tortuous way." The North Vietnamese and NLF were no more prepared than Johnson to abandon their goals, however, and they recognized that unless they were able to maintain a high level of pressure on the United States and South Vietnam, victory would not come at all. Thus while the North Vietnamese accepted American proposals for negotiations, they determined to maintain maximum military pressure. Keeping their main force units out of battle, they sought to sustain small-scale attacks throughout South Vietnam, most of them conducted by paramilitary units.

As a consequence, while in many ways Tet represented a major turning point, it merely elevated the war to a new level of stalemate. During the last eight months of 1968, North Vietnamese and U.S. negotiators met in Paris. Neither was willing to make concessions that would jeopardize achievement of their goals, however, and the negotiations made little progress. When Johnson stopped the bombing of North Vietnam entirely on October 31, the South Vietnamese balked. Fearing that the United States might sell out South Vietnam, the government of Nguyen Van Thieu raised objections that blocked the opening of substantive negotiations until the end of Johnson's term of office.

In the meantime, military activity in South Vietnam grew to unprecedented levels. The air war in South Vietnam reached a new peak of intensity B-52s and fighter-bombers relentlessly attacked infiltration routes, lines of communication, and suspected enemy base camps in South Vietnam and Laos. The number of B-52 attacks tripled in 1968, and the bombs dropped on South Vietnam exceeded one million tons. In the spring and summer, the United States and South Vietnam conducted the largest search-and-destroy missions of the war. The year 1968 was thus the "bloodiest year" of the war, in the words of historian Ronald Spector, and both sides suffered heavy losses. Each could thus claim victory in the campaigns of Tet, but the position of each was also significantly weakened, and neither emerged with sufficient leverage to force a settlement. Tet merely hardened the deadlock, and it would take four more years of "fighting while negotiating" before it was finally broken.

Fighting While Negotiating, 1968–1975

In the aftermath of Tet, the United States and North Vietnam adjusted their strategies to the changed circumstances. After an unsuccessful attempt to win the war through intimidation, the new administration of Richard M. Nixon resorted to a "Vietnamization" strategy designed to hold the line in South Vietnam while easing antiwar pressures at home. In the meantime, Hanoi settled into a classic "fighting while negotiating" strategy, closely coordinating its military, political, and diplomatic moves to maximize pressures on the United States and exacerbate differences between Washington and Saigon.

Certain that they could succeed where their predecessors had failed, Nixon and his national security adviser, Henry A. Kissinger, at first attempted to end the war through threats and diplomacy. The Saigon government appeared stronger than ever in 1969 and with U.S. backing might hang on indefinitely. Nixon and Kissinger also hoped to use the prospect of trade and arms control agreements to secure the Soviet Union's assistance in forcing Hanoi to make major concessions. Comparing his situation to that of Dwight D. Eisenhower with the Korean War in 1953, Nixon concluded that the threat of "massive retaliation" might sway the North Vietnamese, as he believed it had the North Koreans a decade earlier, and he counted on his image as a hard-line anticommunist to make it credible.

In the summer and fall of 1969, Nixon and Kissinger put their plan into action. Through intermediaries, they conveyed to the North Vietnamese their desire for peace and proposed the mutual withdrawal of troops from South Vietnam and restoration of the demilitarized zone. To signal that he meant business, Nixon ordered intensive, secret bombing attacks against North Vietnamese sanctuaries in neutral Cambodia. Publicly, he unveiled what he described as a comprehensive peace plan, revealing proposals he had made privately and then announcing the withdrawal of 25,000 U.S. troops. Through French and Soviet intermediaries, he warned Hanoi that if a settlement were not attained soon he would be compelled to employ "measures of great consequence and force."

Nixon's secret diplomacy and military threats failed to wrench concessions from Hanoi. From the North Vietnamese standpoint, the president's proposals were no better than those of Johnson, and to accept them would be to abandon goals they had been pursuing for nearly a quarter century. Throughout 1968 and into 1969, North Vietnam had tried to sustain maximum military pressure on the United States and South Vietnam, but the results were disappointing. Still hurting from the horrendous losses suffered at Tet but stubbornly clinging to its goals, the leadership reevaluated its strategy. Militarily, it reverted to the defensive and to guerrilla warfare. At the same time, it sought to rebuild the political apparatus in the south so badly damaged by Tet and to drag out the negotiations in a way that would put pressure on the United States to make concessions. Still confident that public opinion would eventually force an American withdrawal from Vietnam, Hanoi ignored Nixon's threats and prepared to wait him out.

"Vietnamization"

His end-the-war strategy frustrated, Nixon fell back on the Vietnamization concept introduced by Johnson on a small scale after Tet. To quiet popular opposition to the war, he initiated a phased withdrawal of U.S. troops and a gradual transfer of primary military responsibility to the South Vietnamese. While U.S. combat forces sought to keep the enemy off balance by relentlessly attacking their supply lines and base areas, American advisers worked frantically to build up and modernize the South Vietnamese armed forces. The force level was increased to more than one million, and the United States turned over to South Vietnam vast quantities of the newest weapons. Nixon hoped that by mobilizing American opinion behind his policies and building up South Vietnam's military strength, he could persuade the North Vietnamese that it would be better to negotiate with him now than with South Vietnam later, and he could extract the concessions necessary to secure an honorable U.S. withdrawal.

In part as a means of supporting Vietnamization, in part to pressure the North Vietnamese, Nixon authorized in April 1970 an invasion of previously neutral Cambodia. The venture backfired. From a purely military standpoint, it achieved modest results, buying some time for Vietnamization. At home, however, the unexpected expansion of a war the president had promised to end enraged his critics, causing massive antiwar demonstrations across the country. The killing of six students during demonstrations at Kent State and Jackson State added to the furor. The Cambodian venture brought the most serious congressional challenge to presidential authority since the beginning of the war. And it merely hardened the diplomatic deadlock. North Vietnamese and NLF delegates boycotted the Paris peace talks until American troops had been withdrawn from Cambodia.

The result was more stalemate. A disastrous ARVN invasion of Laos in 1971 ended in a humiliating retreat back into South Vietnam and made clear that Vietnamization was a long-term undertaking if it could be accomplished at all. Despite continued troop withdrawals, opposition to the war in the United States rose to an all-time high in the summer of 1971. As the purpose of the war became more murky and protest mounted at home, rampant demoralization set in among U.S. troops in Vietnam. Enlisted men refused to obey orders, and "fragging" of officers reached unprecedented proportions. Problems with drugs and racial conflict among G.I.s further highlighted the breakdown of morale. Under these circumstances, Hanoi remained content to bide its time, more and more certain that domestic pressures would eventually force a U.S. withdrawal.

The Easter Offensive

In 1972, each side took measures to break the long-standing stalemate. Since 1969, North Vietnam had carefully built up its resources and man-power for a final military offensive to topple the South Vietnamese regime and force the United States from Vietnam. While attempting to keep Viet-nam on the back burner, Nixon and Kissinger sought to negotiate major changes in U.S. relations with the Soviet Union and China, ensuring the president's reelection, isolating North Vietnam from its major allies and sup-pliers, and leaving it no choice but to come to terms. Neither side would achieve what it hoped with its dramatic moves of 1972, and each would pay a high price trying. But they did bring the war into a final, devastating phase that would ultimately lead to a compromise settlement.

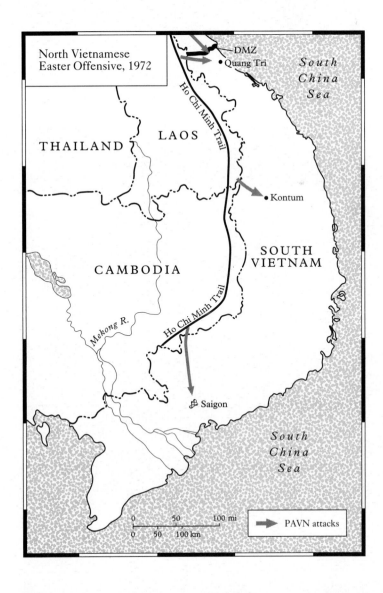

In March 1972, North Vietnam launched a massive, conventional invasion of the south. Hanoi correctly assumed that domestic pressures would prevent Nixon from putting U.S. forces back into Vietnam. The invasion, like that of 1968, was also probably timed to coincide with the presidential campaign in hopes that, as before, a major escalation would produce irresistible pressures for peace in the United States. The North Vietnamese aimed the offensive at the ARVN main force units, hoping to further discredit the Vietnamization policy and leave the countryside open for the NLF.

B-52 Stratofortress bombers played a key role in operations Linebacker and Linebacker II in 1972. A modified B-52D carried as many as 108 500-pound bombs; this bombload almost equaled that of a squadron of B-17s in World War II.

In its first stages, the offensive enjoyed great success. ARVN held off a major assault at An Loc, just sixty miles north of Saigon, but PAVN units forced abandonment of South Vietnamese strongholds at Quang Tri near the demilitarized zone and Kontum in the Central Highlands.

Although stunned by the swiftness and magnitude of the invasion, Nixon responded vigorously. Unwilling to send U.S. troops back to Vietnam, he nevertheless lashed out furiously. He quickly approved B-52 strikes across the demilitarized zone and followed with the most drastic escalation of the war since 1968, the mining of Haiphong harbor, a naval blockade of North Vietnam, and massive, sustained bombing attacks under the code name "Linebacker." The conventional military tactics employed by North Vietnam in the offensive required vast quantities of fuel and ammunition, and the bombing and blockade made resupply extremely difficult. Backed with devastating U.S. air power and fighting the conventional war for which they had been trained, the South Vietnamese stabilized lines in front of Saigon and Hue and even mounted a counteroffensive.

The military campaigns of 1972 raised the stalemate to a new level of violence. Both sides suffered heavily, the North Vietnamese losing an estimated 100,000 men and South Vietnam 25,000, but neither emerged appreciably stronger than before. North Vietnam had demonstrated ARVN's continued vulnerability and the NLF had scored some gains in the countryside, but the South Vietnamese government remained intact and Nixon had not given in. Despite heavy casualties and massive damage from U.S. bombing, the North Vietnamese retained sizable forces in the south, and intelligence reports indicated they could fight on for at least two more years.

Peace and More War, 1973–1975

Thus by the fall of 1972, each side found compelling reasons to compromise. Nixon recognized that an indefinite continuation of the air war might cause serious problems at home. He was eager to uphold earlier promises to end the war, and he wanted a settlement before the election if it could be achieved without embarrassment. North Vietnam had suffered terribly from the latest round of U.S. bombing and also wanted peace if it could be attained without abandonment of long-term goals. Battered, exhausted, and increasingly isolated from its allies, Hanoi apparently concluded that it might get better terms from Nixon before rather than after the election.

Each side thus moved cautiously toward a compromise. The United States had already made a major concession, agreeing to allow North Vietnamese troops to remain in the south after a cease-fire. It also retreated from its absolute commitment to the Thieu regime by agreeing to a tripartite electoral commission that would arrange a political settlement after the cease-fire. In the meantime, the North Vietnamese dropped their insistence on the ouster of Thieu, accepting the principle of a cease-fire that would leave him temporarily in control but would give the NLF status as a political entity in the south. After more than six months of tortuous, on-and-off negotiations, complicated by strenuous objections and obstructionism on the part of the Thieu regime and yet another round of massive bombing of North Vietnam—"Linebacker II," the so-called Christmas bombing—an agreement was signed in January 1973 providing for U.S. military extrication from Vietnam.

The Paris peace agreements did not bring an end to war. The Nixon administration still hoped to keep the Thieu government in power. The United States used various subterfuges to provide continued military assistance to the Saigon government, and civilian advisers assumed the role formerly played by military officials. Both the Thieu government and the North Vietnamese and NLF jockeyed for position in South Vietnam militarily and politically and refused to cooperate in furthering the peace process. Finally, in early 1975, North Vietnam launched another massive military offensive. Without U.S. support, South Vietnam could not withstand the onslaught. Nixon had been forced to resign the previous year because of the Watergate scandals, themselves in part a product of his efforts to control domestic opposition to the war in Vietnam. His successor, Gerald Ford, presiding over a nation traumatized by war-weariness and economic recession, could do nothing. To a large extent America's creation, and never able to stand without massive American support, South Vietnam fell on April 30, 1975, ending a war that in its various phases had lasted for nearly thirty years.

☆   ☆   ☆   ☆

The legacy of Vietnam for warfare was as ambiguous as the war itself. At the tactical level, the utility of the helicopter was validated, and it seemed likely to assume an even greater role in the warfare of the future. The effectiveness of the so-called "smart" bombs first used by the United States in 1972, precisely guided to their targets by computers receiving signals from television cameras and laser beams, foreshadowed a new era in air warfare.

Such new technology failed to produce military success, however, and in the realm of strategy the significance of Vietnam was less certain. Flushed with victory, the Vietnamese hailed the triumph of people over technology, proclaimed the superiority of their revolutionary war doctrines, and heralded a new era in the unrelenting struggle against capitalism. The Vietnamese did wage war with skill and determination, to be sure, and they showed adaptability and even at times genius in conceiving and applying what turned out to be a successful strategy. As Martin van Creveld has observed, moreover, in all the low-intensity wars of the post–World War II era, the less-advanced nation has won, demonstrating the limits of sophisticated weaponry and conventional military forces.

In retrospect, however, the Vietnamese victory appears to owe as much to the unique circumstances of that war and the balance of forces prevailing in Vietnam as to ideology or abstract principles of warfare. Revolutionary war doctrine prevailed nowhere else, and the collapse of the Soviet Union and its eastern European empire less than fifteen years after the fall of Saigon left the Socialist Republic of Vietnam, along with China, North Korea, and Cuba, communist anachronisms in a world dominated by alien political and economic systems. The devastating display of high-technology military weaponry put on by the United States in the Persian Gulf War of 1991 at least called into question simplistic Vietnamese notions that people would always prevail over weapons.

Failure normally provokes more in the way of soul-searching than success, and in the aftermath of their first defeat in war, Americans engaged in an extended and at times agonizing reappraisal of their involvement in Vietnam. Some critics insisted that instead of attempting to wage a conventional war in the guerrilla-war setting of Vietnam, the United States should have recognized the sort of war it was in and employed counterinsurgency methods better designed for it. Others insisted that the United States had failed because timid civilian leaders, by imposing crippling restrictions, had prevented the military from using American power effectively to attain victory. The one thing on which most Americans could agree was that Vietnam had discredited the limited-war doctrines so much in vogue in the 1950s and 1960s. Politicians and military thinkers, liberals and conservatives, all generally concurred in the aftermath of America's failure in Vietnam that limited war was unworkable, even immoral. In going to war in the Persian Gulf in 1991, President George Bush made clear that he would not permit "another Vietnam" and gave his military commanders freedom to use American power swiftly and decisively.

The long-range implications of such conclusions nevertheless remained quite unclear. American success in the Persian Gulf War owed more to the circumstances peculiar to that war than to successful application of lessons from Vietnam. More important, the end of the Cold War eliminated the geopolitical setting in which limited-war doctrines had been conceived and the Vietnam War had been waged. The "lessons" of Vietnam thus remained as murky as the nature of warfare in the post–Cold War world.

SUGGESTED READINGS

Bergerud, Eric. *The Dynamics of Defeat: The Vietnam War in Hau Nghia Province* (Boulder, Col.: Westview Press, 1991).

Clodfelter, Mark. *The Limits of Air Power: The American Bombing of North Vietnam* (New York: Free Press, 1989).

Davidson, Phillip B. *Vietnam at War: The History, 1946–1975* (Novato, Calif.: Presidio Press, 1988).

DeBenedetti, Charles, and Charles Chatfield, assisting author. *An American Ordeal: The Antiwar Movement of the Vietnam Era* (Syracuse, N.Y.: Syracuse University Press, 1990).

Duiker, William.   *The Communist Road to Power in Vietnam* (Boulder, Col.: Westview Press, 1981).

Giap, Vo Nguyen. *People's War; People's Army* (New York: Praeger, 1962).

Herring, George C. *America's Longest War: The United States and Vietnam, 1950–1975* (New York: McGraw-Hill, 1986).

Krepinevich, Andrew. *The Army and Vietnam* (Baltimore: Johns Hopkins University Press, 1986).

Pike, Douglas. *PAVN: People's Army of Vietnam* (Novato, Calif.: Presidio Press, 1986).

———. *Viet Cong* (Cambridge, Mass.: MIT Press, 1966).

Race, Jeffrey. *War Comes to Long An: Revolutionary Conflict in a Vietnamese Province* (Berkeley: University of California Press, 1972).

Sheehan, Neil. *A Bright Shining Lie: John Paul Vann and America in Vietnam* (New York: Random House, 1988).

Spector, Ronald H. *After Tet: The Bloodiest Year in Vietnam* (New York: Free Press, 1993).

Westmoreland, William C. *A Soldier Reports* (Garden City, N.Y.: Doubleday, 1976).

Young, Marilyn B. *The Vietnam Wars, 1945–1990* (New York: HarperCollins, 1990).

4

WAR IN THE MIDDLE EAST: VIOLENCE ACROSS THE SPECTRUM OF CONFLICT

The Arab-Israeli Wars

The Iran-Iraq War

The War in Afghanistan

The Cold War in Retrospect

During the Cold War from 1945 to 1990, wars tended to occur more frequently and to last longer than earlier in the century. By the late 1980s, some thirty-two major and seventy-five minor conflicts were being fought each year at widely varying scales of violence and for reasons often having little or nothing to do with the Cold War. Of the numerous conflicts during the post–World War II period, several of the most significant occurred in the Middle East and Southwest Asia, areas which had long been the scene of religious and ethnic wars. As colonial powers lost their control over this region after 1945, deep-rooted hostilities emerged among the diverse religious and ethnic groups, as well as the newly independent states. With the establishment of the state of Israel in 1948 and a refusal by neighboring Arab states to accept its existence, the region's instability increased. As tensions rose, international interest in the volatile area remained high because of its rich oil reserves and because three of the world's major religions (Islam, Judaism, and Christianity) had their roots in the area. Adding to the region's international importance were its position on the southern flank of the Soviet Union, the presence of Soviet and American client states, and the prominence of the Suez Canal as a vital link between the Red and Mediterranean seas. The strategic importance of the area increased the chances of superpower involvement, but that involvement usually remained indirect given the desire of the superpowers to avoid a direct confrontation and to prevent regional wars from getting out of hand.

The Middle East and Southwest Asia

The presence of advanced weapons and methods added to the significance of conflicts in the Middle East and Southwest Asia. In the post–World War II period, important advances in military technologies produced remarkably accurate and extremely lethal weapons, most notably, a new generation of precision-guided munitions. By the late 1980s, sophisticated electronics and computers promised even greater range, accuracy, and lethality in a wide range of lightweight and rugged weapons. Most of the economies in the Middle East and Southwest Asia had little or no capability to manufacture high-technology weapons and equipment, but foreign arms suppliers, especially the two superpowers, provided the latest arms to the belligerents, often as soon as those arms were fielded. When the superpowers refused to provide the most advanced weapons and equipment, regional powers were able to purchase them elsewhere with vast oil profits. With the employment of precision-guided munitions, medium-range missiles, and chemicals and with the use of constantly changing and improving methods, conflicts in the Middle East and Southwest Asia proved to be crucibles in which the most advanced ideas and technologies were tested and demonstrated.

Despite the numerous wars, continued violence, and active interest of the superpowers in these two regions, conflicts did not spill over into other areas and did not escalate to the point of direct superpower confrontation. Nuclear weapons remained unused, even though the threat of nuclear escalation by the superpowers remained constant. Nonetheless, the combatants often committed their entire populations and resources to the war effort and, in the case of Iraq in the Iran-Iraq War and Russia in the Afghanistan War, used chemical agents against their enemies. Thus, the various conflicts may have been "limited" in the eyes of the superpowers, but to the combatants there was little that was limited about them.

The Arab-Israeli Wars

Of the various conflicts in the Middle East, the Arab-Israeli wars came closest to causing a confrontation of the superpowers. Although the long-term roots of the Arab-Israeli conflict after World War II had little to do with the interests of the superpowers, and although neither superpower desired a confrontation, both provided much equipment and aid to their friends in the region. Many of the tensions stemmed from Jewish efforts to establish an independent state in Palestine and from the Arab rejection of such a state. For nearly two thousand years some Jewish people had yearned to return to the land of their origin and at the end of the nineteenth century began migrating to Palestine. European anti-Semitism in the 1930s and the Nazi Holocaust of World War II increased Jewish migration. The rise of Islam in the seventh century, however, had transformed the Middle East into a predominantly Islamic region, and Jerusalem had become one of Islam's holy cities. Though the Arabs tolerated the return of a small number of Jews to Palestine, they objected to large numbers of Jewish immigrants and rejected the idea of an independent Jewish state in what had become an Arab-Islamic region.

Following World War I and the dismantling of the Ottoman Empire, a League of Nations' mandate gave Great Britain control of Palestine. After World War II, the British reluctantly concluded that they could no longer contain the escalating violence between the Arabs and Jews and turned the problem over to the United Nations, which voted in November 1947 to partition Palestine. This partition intensified the war of guerrillas and terrorists, and savage attacks by both sides increased. When British forces withdrew, the Jews proclaimed on May 14, 1948, the establishment of the state of Israel. Minutes after the establishment of the new state, President Truman announced its recognition by the United States.

The next day Egyptian aircraft struck Tel Aviv, and soon thereafter forces from Egypt, Transjordan, Syria, Lebanon, Iraq, and Saudi Arabia attacked the new state. Most analysts expected the more numerous and better equipped Arabs to defeat the Jews easily. The Arabs, however, delivered a series of poorly coordinated attacks with only part of their forces, and the Israelis committed as many soldiers to battle as the attacking Arabs and fought with great courage and skill. The battles turned out to be a series of disorganized clashes between small units. After four weeks of fighting, both sides accepted a cease-fire sponsored by the United Nations.

Following 1948, tensions between Israelis and Arabs remained high but increased after 1954 when Gamal Abdel Nasser gained control of the Egyptian government. When Nasser's attempts to acquire weapons from the West failed, he turned to the Soviet Union for assistance in modernizing Egyptian forces. A September 1955 agreement between Egypt and Czechoslovakia enabled the Soviets to supply, indirectly, arms to Egypt for the next twenty years. Meanwhile, France objected to Egypt's providing arms to insurgents in Algeria and supplied arms to Israel. Seeking to end the British

presence in Egypt and the Suez Canal zone, Nasser unexpectedly nationalized the Suez Canal on July 27, 1956. The British and French decided to
intervene militarily, and the Israelis joined them in an attack against Egypt.

After calling up reserves on October 28, the Israelis began their
attack against Egypt with a daring airborne landing deep inside the Sinai east
of the Mitla Pass. Concurrent with the landing, a small Israeli force of
infantry and tanks crossed into the Sinai on the southern part of the Israeli
frontier, drove across the desert, and linked up with the paratroopers on
October 30. In the center of the Sinai front, the Israelis moved around the
strong Egyptian defenses at Abu Ageila and attacked them from the rear;
they then drove west toward Bir Gifgafa. In the south, they sent a small column toward Sharm el-Sheikh, the strategic point at the mouth of the Gulf of

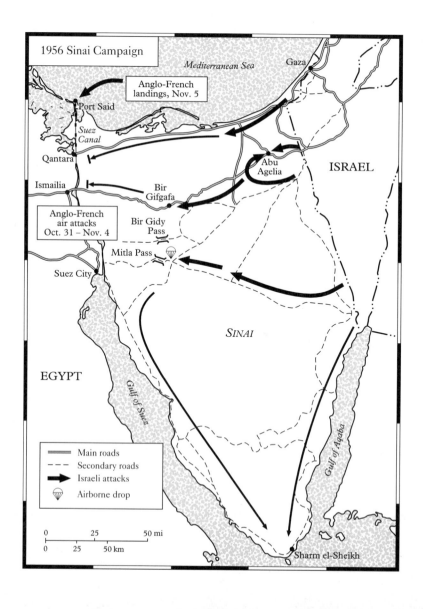

Aqaba. On October 31, French and British bombers began their attacks against Egyptian airfields and destroyed most of the Egyptian air force. Fearing that Egyptian forces in the Sinai would be cut off by the French and British seizure of the Suez Canal, Nasser ordered a withdrawal. Israeli forces eventually halted about fifteen kilometers east of the Suez Canal. As the Israelis expanded their control over the Sinai, the British and the French landed one-and-a-half divisions of infantry on November 6 near the northern mouth of the Suez Canal. After these forces started advancing down the canal, the French and British accepted a United Nations cease-fire.

Despite the decisiveness of the British, French, and Israeli victory, the United States—followed by the Soviet Union—demanded that they relinquish captured Egyptian territory. This was the first and only time the Americans sided with the Soviets against their closest allies. President Eisenhower believed that Western aggression would pressure Third World nations into the Communists' arms and opposed the reassertion by force of colonial control over less-developed nations. He warned the Russians, however, that if they placed troops in the Middle East, the United States would oppose them with force. Reflecting the explosiveness of the situation, a Soviet diplomat stated in a letter to Eisenhower, "If this war is not curbed, it . . . can develop into a third world war." The British, French, and Israelis had no choice but to accede to the American and Soviet demands. In the end, the Israelis withdrew from the territory they had seized, and the British and French lost much of their influence in the region.

Whatever the outcome of the war, the Israelis had developed an effective military force between 1948 and 1956. They organized a small, high-quality standing army always ready for action, and they used universal military conscription of men and women to form reserve units that could be ready for combat in seventy-two hours. With rigorous training and frequent active-duty tours by the reservists, the Israelis prepared their armed forces for extremely demanding operations. The 1956 campaign, however, had not been without difficulties. The Israelis had not forged a clear doctrine on the operations of armor and infantry in mobile warfare and had encountered problems with their loose system of command and control. The Israeli performance had been impressive, but it would be even more so in the future.

1967: The Six-Day War

A fragile peace existed in the Middle East until 1967. A United Nations force patrolled Israel's border on the Sinai and along the Gaza Strip, but along Israel's border with Syria and Jordan, ambushes, firings on civilians, and reprisal raids occurred frequently. The series of events that led to the 1967 war began in early May when Moscow informed Nasser that the Israelis were massing troops for a strike against Syria. Nasser responded to the report—which turned out to be false—by mobilizing his reserves and moving units into the Sinai. He also pressured the United Nations into withdrawing its troops from the Sinai and soon occupied Sharm el-Sheikh, the strategic point at the mouth of the Gulf of Aqaba. As soon as Egyptian units had control of Sharm El-Sheikh, Nasser cut off Israeli shipping through the Gulf of Aqaba, sparking the 1967 war.

The Arabs recognized that the defeat of Israel would require unity. Shortly before the outbreak of hostilities, they established a semblance of unity of command by having the Jordanian king accept an Egyptian general as commander of Arab forces on the Jordanian front. Iraq also permitted its troops to come under Egyptian command; contingents from Kuwait and Algeria joined the Arab forces encircling Israel. Prior to the war, the Arabs—according to an Israeli analyst—had some 250,000 troops, 2,000 tanks, and 700 aircraft available for use against Israel. Despite the nominal authority of the Egyptian general, no true unity of command ruled the diverse forces.

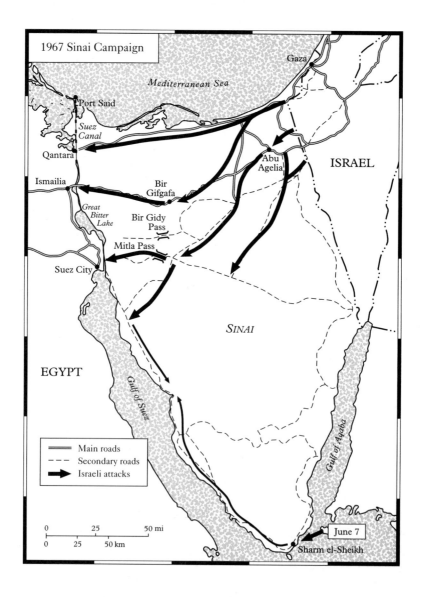

Facing an extremely unfavorable situation but with the advantages of central position, centralized command, and effective intelligence, the Israelis quietly mobilized their reserves to defend against the impending Arab attack and then launched a preemptive air strike. The attack began early on June 5, hit eleven Egyptian airfields, and caught the Arabs completely by surprise. In a matter of hours, the Israelis destroyed most of the Egyptian air force and then turned their attention to the other Arab air forces. By the evening of the second day the Israelis had destroyed more than 400 Arab aircraft, while losing only twenty-six. This remarkable performance provided the Israelis complete air superiority for the remainder of the campaign and was the key to their victory.

Relying on their central position, the Israelis intended to shift forces from one front to another and to defeat Egypt, Jordan, and Syria in turn. The Egyptians were first. In the northern part of the Sinai, an Israeli armored division attacked along the coast and then turned to secure Bir Gifgafa. In the central part of the Sinai, another armored division fought a desperate battle against Egyptian defenses around Abu Ageila and finally managed to capture the main enemy positions. After securing Abu Ageila, armored units raced southwest to secure the Bir Gidy and Mitla passes. By capturing Bir Gifgafa and the Mitla and Bir Gidy passes about fifty kilometers from the Suez Canal, the Israelis trapped most of the Egyptian forces. As the Egyptians attempted to flee, their columns became easy targets for the Israeli Air Force; Nasser later acknowledged that the Egyptian army lost about 80 percent of its equipment in the Sinai. On the fourth day of the war, June 8, some Israeli forces reached the Suez Canal and exchanged artillery and antitank fire with Egyptians across the canal.

On the central front, which included Jerusalem and the West Bank along the Jordan River, Jordan entered the battle around noon on June 5, the day the Israelis' preemptive strike destroyed most of the Arab air forces. Hesitant to cross the border with a sizable assault, the Jordanian army fired artillery and small arms into Israel and crossed the border with a small force south of Jerusalem. The Israelis responded by capturing Jerusalem and then isolating the high ground that runs north of Jerusalem, parallel to the Jordan River valley. After launching attacks on the north and south ends of the high ground, the Israelis gained control of all the bridges over the Jordan River. This cut off the Jordanians on the west bank of the river and ensured their complete defeat.

Having defeated Egypt and Jordan, the Israelis concentrated against the Syrians who had done little to aid their allies in the first days of the war. On the morning of June 9, the Israelis attacked, beginning their efforts with heavy air strikes. Despite strong Syrian fortifications, the Israelis seized the forward slope of the northern Golan Heights by the end of the first day's fighting. The next morning, they fought through the Syrian defenders. To the south of the Sea of Galilee, an Israeli armored division broke through the Syrians, and Israeli paratroopers, using helicopters, assaulted rear positions. As Syrian resistance crumbled, a United Nations cease-fire went into effect at 1830 hours on June 10.

Israeli tanks entered Jerusalem on June 7, 1967. The seizure of the Wailing Wall in the Old City of Jerusalem marked the emotional climax of the war for the Israelis.

Israel's decisive victory changed its strategic situation dramatically. For the first time, it controlled the Golan Heights, the West Bank, and the Sinai; it now had depth for its defense. It also had a very competent air force and army that functioned smoothly together in highly mobile operations. Additionally, the army had developed a strong armored force, improved its command and control system, and polished its methods for attacking fortified positions. Despite some progress, the Arabs still had not coordinated their efforts effectively and had not mastered armored operations. Their piecemeal and tentative attacks had given the Israelis time to mobilize and the opportunity to defeat each opponent in succession. Arab commanders had also displayed less confidence and initiative than their Israeli counterparts.

The 1967 war complicated the Arab-Israeli conflict and brought increased superpower involvement in the region. New controversy focused on the return of the Sinai and the Golan Heights and the status of the West Bank and the Gaza. The Arabs refused to accept the loss of additional territory to the Israelis and began a so-called "War of Attrition" that lasted for three years. This included numerous cross-border raids, artillery barrages, and air strikes. Washington supported Israel's demand for a negotiated peace settlement in exchange for the occupied territories and increased its shipment of arms to Israel. The Soviets also became more involved and agreed to rearm Egypt and Syria; no longer funneling their weapons through Czechoslovakia, they shipped them directly to the Arab states. The discontent of the Arabs uprooted by the establishment and expansion of Israel complicated the situation further. Known as Palestinians, they had formed the Palestine Liberation Organization. Most lived in neighboring Arab states and increasingly used terrorist tactics against the Israelis. Both the Arabs and Israelis soon became weary of the stalemate and casualties, and in August 1970, another cease-fire went into effect.

1973: The Yom Kippur War

After Nasser died in 1970, Anwar Sadat became the president of Egypt. More moderate than his predecessor, he nevertheless felt compelled in October 1973 to go to war against Israel, but he did not seek a decisive defeat of the Israelis. Instead, he sought to break down the aura of Israeli invulnerability. Recognizing that a limited military victory would provide significant political gains, Sadat coordinated his actions effectively with Syria and Jordan so that the Israelis would have to fight a debilitating war of attrition on two fronts.

Sadat also provided his forces with sophisticated weapons and energetically improved their readiness. When the Soviets refused to provide their most advanced weapons, he ordered Soviet advisors out of Egypt. Despite the shock of this expulsion, the Kremlin continued providing weapons, and oil money from other Arab states enabled the Egyptians to purchase arms from different sources. As Sadat worked to improve Egyptian forces, one of his most important steps was to draw officers and soldiers from the better-educated segments of Egyptian society. He recognized the importance of intelligent, well-trained soldiers capable of handling sophisticated weapons. He prepared his army to fight a set-piece battle in which superior numbers of personnel and weapons would wear down the Israelis and brunt the effectiveness of their mobile units.

In the Sinai, Israeli strategy played into the hands of Sadat, primarily because the Israelis had emerged overly confident from their 1967 victory. To defend the Sinai, the Israelis constructed the Bar-Lev line on the east bank of the Suez Canal. They first built huge ridges of sand with a few reaching as high as twenty-five meters. They then prepared small fortified positions every ten to twelve kilometers behind the ridges of sand. The small forces in these positions had the mission of delaying the Egyptians until the Israelis mobilized and deployed sufficient ground forces. Reflecting the prevailing overconfidence, one general officer remarked that the line would be "the Egyptian army's graveyard."

Though Israeli intelligence had performed well in 1967, it did not do so in 1973, and the Egyptian attack surprised the Israelis. As early as October 1, the Israelis had observed increased activity on the western edge of the canal, and on October 2 the commander of the Southern Command ordered a higher state of alert. The Israelis also brought their forces along the Golan Heights to a higher state of readiness. Intelligence officers, however, doubted that the Arab armies would attack during Ramadan, Islam's month of fasting which occurred in October. On the morning of the Arab attack,

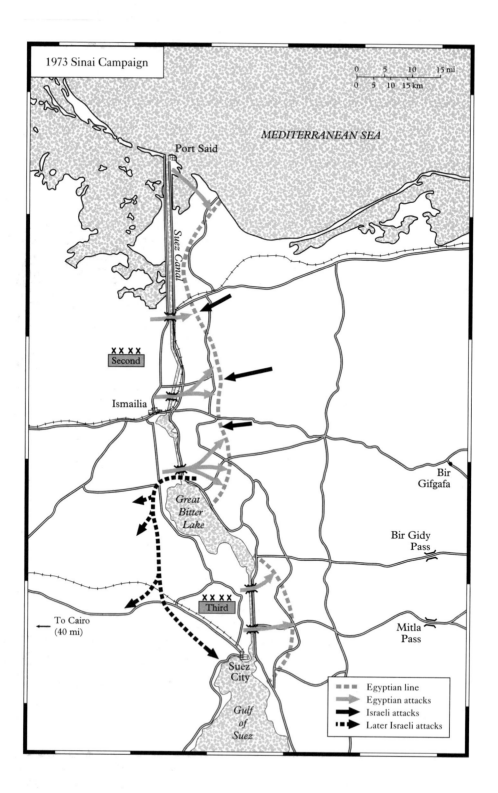

1973 Sinai Campaign

MEDITERRANEAN SEA

Port Said

Suez Canal

XXXX
Second

Ismailia

Bir
Gifgafa

Great
Bitter
Lake

Bir Gidy
Pass

To Cairo
(40 mi)

XXXX
Third

Mitla
Pass

Suez
City

Gulf
of
Suez

Egyptian line
Egyptian attacks
Israeli attacks
Later Israeli attacks

0   5   10   15 mi
0   5   10 15 km

Prime Minister Golda Meir approved a partial mobilization but ruled out a preemptive strike. In the approaching conflict, the Israelis would not have several of the key advantages they had had in 1967.

The Egyptians attacked along the entire front of the canal at 1405 hours on Saturday, October 6, the Jewish Sabbath as well as the Day of Atonement (Yom Kippur). Syria simultaneously struck in the Golan Heights. Preceded by air strikes throughout the Sinai and a huge artillery barrage, five infantry divisions, using about 1,000 rubber assault boats, crossed the Suez Canal. Engineers used high-pressure water hoses to wash away the ridges of sand and open crossing sites through which vehicles could pass; they also began constructing twenty bridges across the canal. After six hours of fighting, the Egyptians had established several bridgeheads with a depth of three to four kilometers. By October 9 the bridgeheads had a depth of about ten to twelve kilometers. Only after consolidating their position across the canal did the Egyptians expect to advance toward Bir Gifgafa and the Mitla and Bir Gidy passes. They intended to remain under the protection of their air defense and repel the expected Israeli armor and air attacks when they came.

The effectiveness of the Arab antiaircraft and antitank defenses shocked the Israelis. During the first week of fighting, the Israelis lost eighty aircraft, about one-quarter of all their front-line planes. With direct Russian participation and assistance, the Egyptians used a variety of surface-to-air missiles to establish an air barrier thirty kilometers wide and 140 kilometers long, along the canal. The Egyptians also beat back three Israeli armored brigades that launched several loosely coordinated attacks without infantry and artillery support. Following the victory of 1967, the Israelis had downplayed the need for infantry and artillery to support armor, and in the first days of the 1973 war, Sagger antitank missiles caused heavy damage to the Israeli tanks. Though awkward to fire, the Sagger had a range of about 3,000 meters and could be manually guided to a target with a hand-controlled stick. For the first time, the individual infantryman had a long-range, highly lethal antitank weapon, and the Israeli tanks found themselves in unfavorable circumstances without infantry and artillery support in a combined-arms team.

On Sunday, October 14, the Egyptians charged out of their bridgeheads in six major thrusts. In the subsequent battle, about 2,000 tanks on both sides fought the largest tank battle since Kursk in 1943. Though the Egyptians penetrated about fifteen to eighteen kilometers, they lost about 200 tanks. Instead of making one or two strong armored thrusts, they diluted the effect of their offensive by splitting their forces into six weaker efforts. Perhaps more important, the Egyptians moved outside the umbrella of their highly effective air defenses and suffered heavily from Israeli air strikes. They also encountered Israelis armed with newly arrived TOW (tube-launched, optically tracked, wire-guided) antitank missiles from the United States.

As soon as the opportunity appeared, the Israelis went on the offensive. At 1700 hours on October 15, the Israelis began a daring and bold operation to cross the Suez Canal north of the Great Bitter Lake. Brigadier

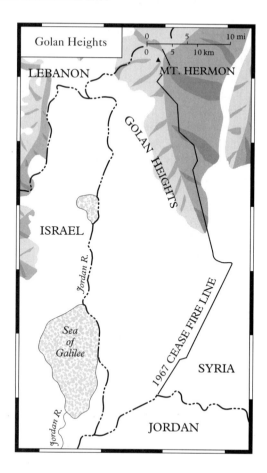

General Ariel Sharon's division cleared a corridor through the Egyptian forces on the east bank of the canal. Despite fierce fighting, the division crossed the canal and caused pandemonium among several Egyptian divisions that were surprised by its sudden appearance. As Sharon's division began expanding the bridgehead to the west of the canal, elements from two additional Israeli divisions crossed the canal. These forces destroyed air-defense sites on the west bank of the canal and thereby enabled the Israeli Air Force to operate more effectively. In addition to threatening the logistical support of the entire Egyptian army, the three divisions turned south and cut off the Egyptian Third Army, which was on the eastern bank of the canal.

Though huge forces participated in the Sinai action, some of the most critical fighting occurred on the Golan Heights, where the Israelis had very little space to trade for time. The Israelis initially had only two infantry battalions in the Golan Heights, reinforced by two tank battalions from the 188th (Barak) Brigade. In late September, the 7th Armored Brigade arrived, bringing the total number of tanks to about 175. On October 6 three Syrian mechanized divisions, reinforced by two armored divisions, attacked these small forces, which had to hold until reinforcements rushed to their assistance. With about 1,500 tanks, the Syrians greatly outnumbered the Israelis. During the desperate fighting, which lasted for three days and two nights without respite, the Israelis threw newly mobilized squads, platoons, and companies into the battle as soon as they arrived on the front. Israeli and Syrian units became intermingled, and artillery from both sides pounded the battlefield continuously. Despite the odds, the Israelis halted the Syrians, and by October 10 had driven them behind the 1967 truce line. The Syrians lost almost 900 tanks and hundreds of weapons and vehicles.

On October 11 the Israelis attacked Syria. Despite heavy losses, units from the 188th and 7th brigades led the attack. On the morning of October 13, the Israelis destroyed most of an Iraqi armored brigade that was attempting to reinforce the Syrians. That night, the Israelis punched through enemy defenses along the main Damascus road. Although a combination of Syrian, Jordanian, and Iraqi forces made several counterattacks, they failed to crack the Israeli positions. On October 22 the Israelis captured Mount Hermon on the northern end of the Golan Heights, but it was clear that any further advance into Syria would stretch Israeli logistical support beyond its limits and provoke an even stronger reaction from the Arabs.

As the Israeli victory became apparent, the United States and the Soviet Union called for an end to the fighting; even though Israel and Egypt agreed to a cease-fire, the fighting continued. Fearful of a complete destruction of Arab forces, the Soviet Union threatened to act "unilaterally" and to send in troops to enforce a cease-fire. This provoked a worldwide alert for U.S. armed forces; the crisis passed when Moscow agreed to an international peacekeeping force without American or Soviet participation. On October 24, the day prior to the alert of American forces, the Israelis reluctantly accepted a cease-fire. Despite overwhelmingly unfavorable odds, they had won a remarkable victory. As in the earlier Arab-Israeli wars, the key was their aggressive, highly mobile, hard-hitting style of fighting that placed a special premium on individual initiative.

Though the Israelis had won the war, Sadat had achieved his strategic objective of destroying the aura of Israeli invulnerability. As many as 12,000 soldiers from both sides lost their lives in the 1973 war, and Egypt and Syria lost about 2,000 tanks and 500 aircraft. Despite these losses, many Arabs believed they had won an important psychological victory. Their near-success demonstrated how some of them—particularly the Egyptians—had improved their loosely coordinated, oftentimes tentative style of fighting that had characterized earlier wars. Although the Israelis had gained territory on the Golan Heights and had halted only one hundred kilometers from Cairo, they had suffered a relatively large number of casualties (almost 3,000 killed), paid a high economic cost, and seen their regional and international position weakened at the expense of the Arabs. Their margin of victory would have been narrower if the United States had not rushed weapons and supplies to them.

Subsequent events also confirmed the reliance of the United States, Western Europe, and Japan on Middle Eastern oil and the utility of oil as a weapon to influence their behavior. To punish Israel's supporters, Arab members of the Organization of Petroleum Exporting Countries shut off the flow of oil in 1973 to the United States and the Netherlands (which had permitted the shipment of American military supplies to Israel across its territory). Though brief, the oil embargo demonstrated that whatever the outcome of future battles, the Arab countries had a powerful means to influence Western political priorities.

Following the 1973 war, the Camp David Accords of September 1978 provided for the establishment of normal relations between Egypt and Israel and resulted in the signing of a peace treaty between the two states in March 1979. The peace treaty caused great anguish among the other Arab states and did not solve the intractable problem of the Palestinians. The Palestine Liberation Organization (PLO) exercised considerable influence among the large numbers of Palestinian refugees in Lebanon. More a revolutionary military force than a classic military force, the PLO relied on subversion, kidnappings, and terrorism. With the presence of the PLO exacerbating relations in an already splintered society, a civil war erupted in Lebanon in early 1975. Responding to terrorist attacks, the Israelis launched air strikes and commando raids into Lebanon and in March 1978 and June 1982 invaded southern Lebanon. Thus even though Egypt and Israel established normal relations after the 1973 war, violence between the Arabs and Israelis did not end, and strife continued on Israel's northern border.

Between 1948 and 1973, the waging of war had changed dramatically in the Middle East. While the belligerents in 1948 engaged in numerous small, disorganized battles, the battles and campaigns of the 1956, 1967, and 1973 wars became larger, more complicated, and more sophisticated. For the extremely mobile campaigns of these wars, the Israelis were the first to recognize the need for high-quality leaders, capable of using their initiative and acting independently, but the Arab forces, particularly the Egyptians, slowly improved their forces. Nonetheless, the Arabs never displayed the flexibility and daring of the Israelis; they also never had unity of command. In each of the successive wars the combatants used increasingly complex and sophisticated weaponry. The 1967 campaign, in particular, demonstrated the remarkable ability of the Israelis to integrate air and ground operations and to wage mobile warfare reminiscent of the German *Blitzkrieg* of World War II. In 1973 about 2,000 tanks on both sides became engaged in the largest tank battle since Kursk in 1943. As is evident from Israeli successes in 1967 and 1973, they mastered armored operations before their opponents and employed their air and ground units in a more tightly coordinated and effective fashion; they also rapidly adapted to the requirement for combined-arms teams. The Egyptians, however, achieved great surprise with their use of precision-guided munitions and highly effective air-defense weapons in the 1973 war. Given the Middle East's strategic importance and the sophistication of the weapons employed, military leaders throughout the world carefully studied the Arab-Israeli wars for insights into how warfare was evolving and, particularly after the 1973 war, used that conflict as a benchmark to measure the readiness of their own forces.

The Iran-Iraq War

Another significant war in the Middle East and Southwest Asia during the Cold War was the Iran-Iraq War of 1980–1988. Though superpower involvement was limited, Iran and Iraq devoted their entire efforts to what was for them a total war without nuclear weapons. The fighting included a curious mixture of high-technology weapons and gruesomely bloody infantry assaults that seemed more appropriate for 1914 than for 1980. For the first time since World War I, chemicals were widely used, and for the first time since World War II, heavy aerial attacks hit population and economic centers. The Iraqis, having assembled a huge arsenal of modern weaponry, maintained an edge in the quality of their weapons, but the willingness of the Iranians to die for their nation and their religion enabled them to overcome significant disadvantages. The professionalism of the operations and the quality of generalship on both sides, however, were inferior to those of the Israelis in the Arab-Israeli wars.

The Iran-Iraq War stemmed from many centuries of religious (Sunni vs. Shi'ite) and ethnic (Persian vs. Arab) conflict, but President Saddam Hussein of Iraq attacked Iran for more immediate reasons. Concerned about Iran's efforts to undermine his regime, he hoped to curtail the spread of Islamic fundamentalism to which Iraq's Shi'ite population seemed particularly vulnerable. Seeking to increase his influence over the Persian Gulf area, he also wanted to seize key geographic areas that would enhance the political and economic power of Iraq.

Optimistic because of accounts of political, economic, and military turmoil in Iran, Saddam evidently expected a short, limited war. His confidence stemmed from the vast sums he had spent improving his armed forces and equipping them with more than 1,700 Soviet T-54, T-55, and T-62 tanks, 1,800 armored personnel carriers, and 340 combat aircraft. Saddam also knew that Iran had been weakened by the upheaval of its 1979 Islamic revolution and by the chaos engendered by Ayatollah Ruhollah Khomeini's efforts to subordinate Iranian political and military power to Islamic fundamentalists. As part of U.S. containment policy, the Americans had built up Iranian forces in the post–World War II period, but following the Islamic overthrow of the Shah of Iran, Khomeini had severely reduced the size of the Iranian armed forces, while dramatically increasing the number of militia and simultaneously replacing scores of officers with religious leaders who had little or no military experience. Despite Saddam's expectations of a quick and easy victory, the war would drag on for years and ultimately would cause somewhere between 600,000 and 970,000 deaths.

After a surprise air attack against ten Iranian air fields on September 22, 1980, the Iraqis launched ground attacks into Iran along four separate axes. Because many of Iran's most advanced planes were in protective hangars, the preemptive aerial attack failed to yield any real advantages. The ground attack also produced little, and about one week after the invasion began, Saddam called for a cease-fire. The Iraqis attempted several

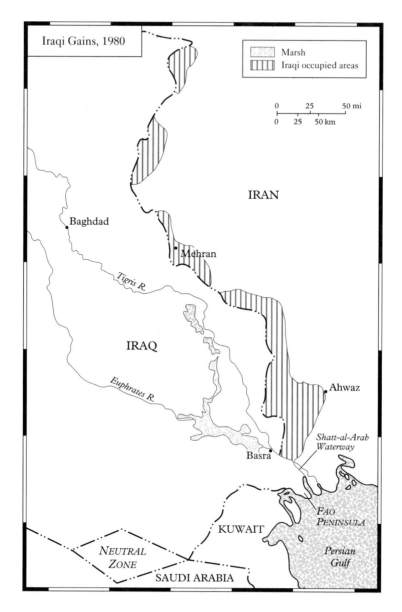

subsequent attacks, but by March 1981 they had exhausted themselves. The attacks had gained little more than a narrow strip of Iranian territory along the 1,100-kilometer border. Instead of giving the Iraqis an important strategic advantage or a swift victory, the attacks provided the revolutionary regime in Teheran with a rallying cry for the mobilization of its people. A huge outpouring of patriotism and fury brought forth thousands of volunteers willing to die for their nation and the Islamic faith. Having failed to win a swift victory, the Iraqis struggled to avoid defeat and survive against Iran's far greater population and resources. Optimistic hopes for a short, limited war were replaced by the dreadful specter of a long war involving all of Iraq's population and resources.

As governments throughout the world watched the unfolding events, many feared the spread of Ayatollah Khomeini's influence in the Middle East more than Saddam's record of aggression and human rights abuses. Consequently, most members of the international community refused to sell Iran arms and equipment even though Saddam had initiated the war. The lack of international support caused the Iranians significant logistical problems for the remainder of the war. In particular, the inability to obtain repair parts quickly decreased the combat effectiveness of their air force.

From September 1981 through May 1982, Iran seized the initiative with a series of poorly coordinated and executed attacks. The inferior quality of its operations came from its inadequately trained commanders and staffs and its shortage of equipment. In some cases, the Iranians used human wave attacks. These attacks sometimes began with hundreds of children and old men, motivated by religious fervor, racing forward and using their bodies to detonate concealed mines. Then waves of poorly trained militia threw themselves on the barbed wire and attempted to cut the wire while under the fire of the Iraqis. Finally, better equipped and trained soldiers attacked over the mangled bodies of the initial waves of children, old men, and militia.

Iranian leaders hoped the religious zeal and nationalism of their people would enable them to expel the invaders, but such emotions did not overcome serious organizational and operational weaknesses. As Iranian commanders and staffs gained experience and became more effective, they used other methods such as the launching of night infantry assaults, supported by tanks and attack helicopters. Despite huge losses, the Iranians pushed the Iraqis back. At the end of June 1982 Saddam Hussein ordered the evacuation of most of the territory seized from Iran. This withdrawal, however, did not end hostilities, and Iran soon shifted from attempting to drive the invaders from its territory to defeating Iraq and deposing Saddam.

In July, the Iranians launched a huge offensive to capture Basra, Iraq's second largest city. After this attack failed, they began an offensive in October 1982 on the central front, seeking to drive toward Baghdad. Other attacks along the long front followed, but strong Iraqi defenses held the Iranians to relatively insignificant gains. By December 1982, the Iraqis were using limited amounts of mustard gas to repel night attacks and disrupt human wave assaults. They may also have used nerve gas. One Iraqi general officer compared the use of chemicals against the Iranians to the use of "pesticides" against "insects." Despite huge losses and no significant gains, the Iranians continued to press forward.

The war entered a new phase in 1984 when Saddam began using his superior air power to halt the shipment of Iranian oil through the Persian Gulf. In February, Iraq launched attacks on the Kharg oil terminal in the Gulf, and in subsequent weeks attacked several tankers with Exocet air-to-surface cruise missiles. Since the Iraqis shipped their oil by pipeline, mainly through Turkey, the Iranians could not attack Iraqi tankers, but they could attack the shipping of Iraq's allies, Kuwait and Saudi Arabia. Subsequent attacks against tankers were condemned by the United Nations' Security Council and began what came to be known as the "Tanker War." Throughout the remainder of 1984, attacks on commercial shipping and population centers continued. While Iran held the initiative on the ground, Iraq controlled the skies, and oil from Iraq and its allies continued to flow to the outside world.

From March to June 1985, the "War of the Cities" occurred. As early as 1980–1981, Iraq had used Frog 7A missiles against Iranian cities and in 1982 began using Scud missiles (a NATO code name for the Soviet-designed SS-1 missile). In 1985, however, Iraq intensified its attacks, including more than forty air strikes against Teheran. After Iran acquired its own Scud missiles from Libya, it too began firing missiles at Iraq's cities, mainly Baghdad. Both sides improved their tactics in 1984 and 1985, but no dramatic changes occurred. In early 1986 improvements in the quality of Iranian commanders and staffs enabled them to launch two major offensives simultaneously for the first time in the war. They made one attack north of Basra and the other in the Fao peninsula, to the west of the Shatt-al-Arab waterway. Despite strong Iraqi counterattacks, the Iranians clung to the Fao peninsula and severed Iraq's direct access to the Persian Gulf. The impression that things were going badly for Baghdad was heightened when an Iraqi offensive in May against Mehran in the central sector was driven back in July with heavy losses. Saddam had little choice but to intensify air attacks.

The key development in 1987 was the increasingly active role played by the United States. Washington reluctantly concluded that an Iranian victory was contrary to its interests and threatened the stability of the Middle East. After Kuwait transferred ownership of half its tankers to a U.S. shipping company, American warships began providing them security in the Persian Gulf. In May an Iraqi aircraft launched two Exocet cruise missiles—

The Exocet missile proved deadly against ships in the Falklands and in the Persian Gulf conflicts. The missile had a range of thirty-five to forty miles, and a pilot could launch a missile toward a target ship without making visual contact. After being launched, the missile traveled to its target only six to ten feet above the water at a speed of more than 600 miles an hour.

supposedly accidentally—against the USS *Stark*, killing thirty-seven crewmen and badly damaging the ship. When a tanker escorted by three U.S. warships hit a mine on July 22, a direct U.S.-Iran naval confrontation occurred. American forces made several attacks, including one against an Iranian gunboat laying mines and another against two offshore platforms being used as bases for Iranian gunboats. By the end of 1987, the United States had over thirty warships (but no aircraft carriers) in the Gulf, and Iran confronted the possibility of even greater American involvement.

In 1988 the strategic situation began to favor Iraq. The early part of that year brought a lull in the fighting, primarily because the Iranians could not mount their usual offensive. Increasing domestic discontent with the war hampered the mustering of sufficient forces. As the Iranians began to weaken, Iraq escalated its aerial attacks on Iranian cities. An important offensive occurred in the Fao peninsula on the night of April 16 when the Iraqis pushed the Iranians across the Shatt-al-Arab waterway. Iran's concerns were heightened by U.S. Navy attacks on April 18 that sank two of Iran's four frigates and one of its armed speedboats. These attacks forced Iran to confront the awful possibility of having to fight Iraq and a superpower at the same time.

Beginning in May, Saddam launched offensives in the north and central sectors, and then in the south. Perhaps more ominously for the Iranians, the Iraqis attacked at dawn in June against the southern part of the Haur-al-Hawizeh marshes. In addition to dropping airborne troops inside Iran, the Iraqis mounted an amphibious attack with Hovercraft. In about a day, they won one of their most important victories, but they soon withdrew from the captured territory. Saddam evidently sought to signal the Iranians his willingness to end the war.

Amidst the background of an increasingly bleak situation for the Iranians, the USS *Vincennes* mistakenly identified an Iranian airplane with 290 people aboard as a war plane and shot it down. The downing of the civilian aircraft sapped the morale of Iranian leaders, for it signaled the possibility of increased superpower involvement in the war. At the same time Iran experienced even more formidable problems in obtaining military supplies from other countries and adequately equipping its armed forces. Mismanagement and corruption magnified the effect of the international community's refusal to provide arms, spare parts, and supplies.

In late July, the Iraqis attacked in the northern, central, and southern sectors. In one case they penetrated more than sixty kilometers into Iran and came within twenty-five kilometers of a provincial capital, making it clear that they had the initiative on the ground and in the air. The Iranians managed to regain their lost territory by July 25, primarily through the use of human wave attacks. Unlike the initial outpouring of volunteers in 1980, however, the Iranians came forward less willingly. As Iran's situation became more desperate, cracks began to appear in Khomeini's tight control.

Having no real alternative, Iran finally accepted a truce. At 0300 hours on August 20, 1988, the long war ended. For years the war had provided Iranian leaders the opportunity to consolidate and expand the Islamic revolution, but the possibility of losing on the battlefield threatened the revolution's existence. In the end, neither country gained from the long and bitter war, and both plundered their economies and wasted thousands of lives. Some analysts, aware of the long enmity between the two countries and of the inconclusive ending of the war, wondered when it would resume.

The war itself witnessed few innovations, but the Iraqis used the latest chemicals, missiles, and high-technology weapons. They relied on their superior air power to attack Iranian cities and halt the shipment of Iranian oil through the Persian Gulf. They also integrated rudimentary airborne and amphibious operations into their campaigns, particularly in the latter part of the war. Nevertheless, neither Iraq nor Iran demonstrated a high level of operational proficiency during the war, though both did slowly improve their performance. When the United States became involved, the Americans' advanced naval weapons and methods dominated the Persian Gulf, but the damaging of the USS *Stark* by Iraqi Exocet missiles and the downing of the Iranian civilian airplane by a missile from the USS *Vincennes* demonstrated the complexities and dangers of employing such weapons in combat. In the broadest sense, however, the nature of the war and its place within the history of warfare is suggested more by the Iranians' human-wave attacks than by high-technology weapons or sophisticated operations.

The War in Afghanistan

A different type of war occurred in Afghanistan where Afghan guerrillas fought the Soviets from 1979–1988. For many reasons, the war bears a closer resemblance to the Vietnam War than to other conflicts in the Middle East and Southwest Asia. Strategically located between Russia, Persia (Iran), and India, Afghanistan had long been the scene of international conflict and intrigue, even though it was a backward, divided country with numerous quarrelsome tribes. A new conflict began in April 1978 with the overthrow of the government of Mahammed Daoud (who had overthrown the monarchy in 1973) and the seizure of power by the People's Democratic Party of Afghanistan. Armed resistance against the new Marxist government broke out quickly, and the situation deteriorated steadily, particularly when the ruling government split into factions openly contending for power. In December 1979, the Soviets, concerned about the key region on their southern border, supported a coup. While Soviet units already in Kabul seized control of key sites, two swiftly moving columns crossed the border, traveled along traditional invasion routes, reinforced the Soviet units already in Afghanistan, and seized important provincial cities. These actions neutralized the Afghan armed forces, established Soviet control over major urban centers, and enabled the Soviets to install Babrak Karmal as president of the Democratic Republic of Afghanistan (DRA). Some Afghan units resisted, but the Soviets disarmed them quickly.

Though hoping for a quick collapse of resistance similar to Czechoslovakia in 1968, the Soviets provoked a struggle that lasted until 1988 and

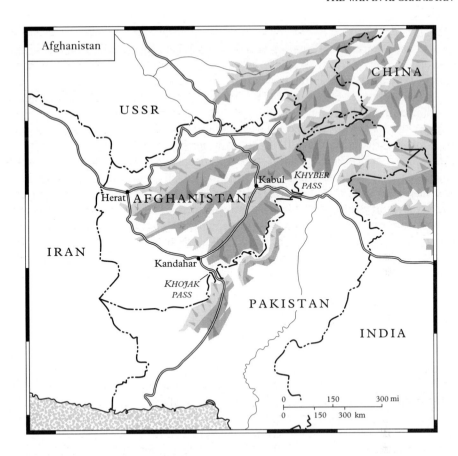

pitted regular troops and advanced technology against divided bands of guerrillas operating out of difficult mountainous terrain. Initially the Soviets were not overly concerned about Afghan resistance. The 15 million people living in Afghanistan seemed miniscule in comparison to the 265 million people in the Soviet Union and their vast industrial and military power. Soviet military leaders believed the various Afghan tribes had little unity and had only obsolete rifles and equipment left over from World War II. They did not anticipate the fierce resistance to Karmal's government from numerous factions of Afghan guerrillas, or Mujahideen. They also overlooked the Afghans' traditional hatred for foreign interference and the disastrous experience of the British in 1842 and 1879–1880.

During the first four years of the war, the Soviets and their Afghan allies held the major urban centers and launched attacks against the Mujahideen in remote and often mountainous areas. Opposition increased during this period as more than half of the 80,000 soldiers in the Afghan army deserted or joined the Mujahideen; many of the deserters brought their weapons with them. Relying on classic guerrilla tactics, the Mujahideen made numerous small-scale attacks and conducted ambushes of Soviet and DRA convoys along the major roads. Along with their indomitable fighting spirit, which was partially sustained by a wide wave of Islamic fundamentalism, the

Mujahideen possessed one other very important advantage—their ability to use sanctuaries in Pakistan and Iran as bases for support and training. Bands of guerrillas crossed the border with impunity and struck without warning throughout Afghanistan.

The initial Soviet and DRA tactics relied on standard techniques of mechanized warfare—a preliminary bombardment from artillery, helicopters, and airplanes, followed by a ground assault with tanks and armored personnel carriers. Especially in the first years of the war, Soviet and DRA forces often conducted division-sized offensives against Mujahideen sanctuaries. They also used large cordon and search operations in which they encircled an area and then combed it thoroughly for the elusive guerrillas. Particularly in the central and eastern portions of Afghanistan, however, the guerrillas found many hiding places among the rocks, crevices, and valleys of the rugged countryside. With their detailed knowledge of the area, they could operate easily in the mountainous areas and were not confined to the roads, but the Soviets usually had to move by helicopter or use road-bound vehicles.

Within months after arriving in Afghanistan, the Soviets slowly began modifying the structure of their units and changing their tactics. When they first intervened in Afghanistan, they employed an airborne division and four motorized rifle divisions, but they soon discovered that mechanized units and conventional attacks did not yield substantial success. They turned to decentralized, mobile operations with battalions and regiments reinforced by artillery, engineers, and helicopters. They also quickly increased their helicopters and trained their infantry for heliborne operations. Though still relying on mechanized infantry, they used air-transported infantry to strike swiftly at unsuspecting Afghan guerrillas. As time passed, their airmobile tactics resembled those employed by the Americans in Vietnam.

As the Soviets and DRA modified their organizations and tactics, the Mujahideen began receiving weapons from the west, including mines, recoilless rifles, and small antiaircraft guns. Though some unity of command would have ensured better coordination and perhaps greater effectiveness, most of the guerrilla factions operated independently. They moved back and forth across the border from Pakistan and Iran and launched operations with virtually no strategic or tactical purpose other than the killing of Soviet soldiers and their supporters. Rocket attacks against Kabul and other important cities became a standard practice. To starve and terrorize the guerrillas into submission, the Soviets used "scorched earth" tactics and destroyed villages and crops. They also used chemicals, particularly in the first three years of the war, but the Mujahideen stubbornly continued to resist and despite heavy losses controlled significant parts of Afghanistan.

By 1984 the Soviets had to choose between a massive increase in forces or a different strategy. Reluctant to accept higher casualties and to increase the size of their forces beyond 125–140,000, they adopted a different strategy. They shifted from destroying individual guerrillas to destroying the infrastructure needed by the guerrillas for survival and to disrupting their supply lines and bases in border provinces. To accomplish this, they attacked the supply lines along which men and equipment flowed from Pakistan; they also unleashed attacks against areas in the border provinces that previously had been sanctuaries for the guerrillas. Air and artillery strikes against hostile population centers became routine. Soviet troops attacked villages suspected of having sheltered guerrillas and destroyed their livestock and crops. For a time the Soviet and DRA forces seemed to have gained the upper hand. As attacks against villages increased in frequency and destruction, more and more Afghans fled Afghanistan. Analysts estimated that about 30–50 percent of the populace had departed by 1986. Nonetheless, the Soviets and DRA still had little control outside the urban centers.

In 1986, it became more and more apparent that battlefield victories and ruthless destruction of civilians and their property could not destroy the insurgents' will to fight. New air-defense weapons also began to have a significant effect. As early as February 1982, the Mujahideen had used the SAM-7 surface-to-air missile against Soviet aircraft, but in February 1986 the United States decided to send high-technology weapons to Afghanistan. By mid-1987 the Soviets were losing about one aircraft per day to shoulder-fired air-defense missiles, particularly the American-made Stinger. They quickly learned that aircraft had to take evasive measures and could not operate effectively near guerrilla units armed with the highly effective air-defense weapons.

The disruption of aerial operations reduced the Soviets' freedom to maneuver and forced them to launch ground attacks with less air support and fewer heliborne assaults. In 1987 and 1988, most operations reverted to reliance on mechanized infantry formations, supported by artillery. In

The first 340 Stinger missiles fired by Afghan rebels brought down 269 Soviet aircraft. These losses forced the Soviets to change their aviation tactics completely.

reality, the Soviets no longer had the mobility of the lightly equipped Afghan guerrillas. In November 1988, they began using Scud missiles— despite their inaccuracy—to provide fire support for units and to increase terror among the Afghan people. As the mobility of the Soviets decreased, they reluctantly withdrew from many remote areas and sought to secure urban areas, thereby permitting the Mujahideen slowly to gain the upper hand. The Mujahideen began using trucks rather than pack animals and main roads rather than trails. They also began using heavier weapons.

Karmal's presidency ended in November 1986. His replacement, Mohammed Najibullah, head of the secret police, adopted a more Islamic public image in November 1987 in an attempt to sway the Mujahideen. Though under Soviet control, he made another attempt at "national recon- ciliation" by dropping the word "democratic," which supposedly suggested Marxist leanings, and adopting the name, Republic of Afghanistan.

Continuing to search for alternatives, the Soviets and their Afghan allies launched air raids against Mujahideen bases in Pakistan. They stepped up attacks on villages controlled by guerillas and air-dropped thousands of mines along suspected supply routes. Despite these last-ditch efforts, the strategic initiative had shifted to the Mujahideen. The Soviet and Afghan forces still lacked popular support, and they had little control outside the major urban centers. In early 1988, the Mujahideen estimated that they controlled 80 percent of the countryside. Battlefield victories by the Soviets and heavy casualties among the Afghan people had neither ended the flow of troops and supplies across the border nor increased popular support for the new government. The deteriorating Soviet situation worsened as soldiers' morale dropped, discipline dwindled, and drug use became more prevalent.

Like the Americans after the Tet Offensive in Vietnam, the Soviets refused to increase the number of forces involved in the war. Facing over- whelming economic problems at home, they finally decided to withdraw. After signing an accord in Geneva in April 1988, they staged a farewell parade in Kabul in May and began to transfer equipment to the Kabul gov- ernment and withdraw Soviet troops. The last Soviet soldiers departed Afghanistan on February 15, 1989. With the Cold War ending and the Soviet empire disintegrating, the government in Kabul remained faithful to the Soviets, and the war continued even though the Afghans were now fight- ing a civil war among themselves.

In April 1992, fourteen years after the Soviet-backed coup plunged Afghanistan into war, Najibullah gave up power, tried to flee, and ended up seeking refuge in a United Nations' building. As thousands of Mujahideen poured into Kabul, rival factions fought for control over the Afghan capital. An uneasy truce finally emerged, but factional strife—ethnic, tribal, and reli- gious—continued. The outlook for Afghanistan remained bleak.

In the Afghanistan War, the Russians experienced numerous difficul- ties as they initially attempted to fight the Mujahideen with forces designed for combat in central Europe. Even after changing their methods and rely- ing more on airmobile operations, the Russians failed to defeat the highly mobile Mujahideen and found themselves at a disadvantage when shoulder-fired air-defense weapons destroyed many of their aircraft and restricted the role of air support. Though facing defeat, the Russians refused to expand the war significantly in order to end the flow of weapons and supplies to the Mujahideen. In the end, the Russians limited their forces and objectives and by exercising self-restraint chose defeat rather than escalation.

The Cold War in Retrospect

The most unique aspect of the Cold War was the role played by nuclear weapons. From the dropping of the first atomic bomb in August 1945 to the formal dissolving of the Warsaw Pact in July 1991, atomic and then nuclear weapons exercised a dramatic influence over national security policy, military strategy, and the organizations and equipment of military forces. The influence of nuclear weapons over national security policy expanded as technological advances extended the range, improved the accuracy, and increased the payloads of nuclear delivery systems, vastly multiplying the destructive power of nuclear devices. Many changes in the nuclear era came from one of the superpowers reacting to actions or advances by the other. After the Soviet Union exploded an atomic and then a nuclear device, the Americans lost their monopoly over nuclear weapons, and deterrence became crucially important, particularly as Soviet nuclear forces approached parity with those of the Americans. Foremost among other factors influencing questions relating to nuclear weapons were concerns about the morality of destroying millions of people, military and civilian. To many critics, the acronym for Mutual Assured Destruction, MAD, aptly described the reasoning, or lack thereof, that underpinned theories relating to nuclear warfare. Nonetheless, changes in ideas and technologies pertaining to nuclear weapons greatly influenced the policies, strategies, and forces of both sides during the Cold War.

One of the most important consequences of the introduction of nuclear arms was the opening of an era of limited war. Throughout the Cold War, both the Americans and the Soviets feared the consequences of nuclear escalation and sometimes found themselves having to yield or compromise rather than raise the stakes in a crisis. Though both sides sought advantages in regional conflicts, neither wanted a crisis to draw the superpowers into a direct confrontation. Aware of the dangers of escalation and nuclear warfare, political and military leaders acknowledged the existence of various levels of conflict, ranging from low-intensity, to mid-intensity, to high-intensity, to general nuclear war. To avoid general nuclear war or high-intensity conflict (which presumably could escalate quickly), the superpowers limited their objectives or the size and nature of their military forces involved in a conflict. Nevertheless, both devoted considerable resources and efforts to the development of new weapons and methods, and both sold or shared these with friendly or client states. As a result, modern arms spread around the world at an unprecedented rate, and regular and irregular forces used them with terrifying effect in some 160 major conflicts and numerous minor ones between 1945 and 1990.

Though the superpowers avoided a direct confrontation, numerous revolutionary wars occurred in the post–World War II decades as European colonial empires dissolved and new successor states appeared. After Mao and the Communists successfully seized power in China in 1949, Mao's ideas wielded great influence. Along with other leaders such as Ho Chi Minh, he recognized the difficulty of achieving a quick victory against better-armed opponents, so he placed equal emphasis on political and military efforts and relied on a protracted struggle to exhaust his enemies and permit the seizure of power. In the ensuing decades of violence, dealing with guerrillas became not only the most common but also one of the most complex aspects of the Cold War. Amidst increased concern about low-intensity conflict in protracted wars, military forces developed special expertise and capabilities to deal with guerrillas. The Americans learned hard lessons about guerrilla warfare in Vietnam, while the Soviets learned similar lessons against the Mujahideen in Afghanistan.

Terrorism also became common. Though radicals had long used sustained, clandestine violence—murders, kidnappings, bombings, skyjackings—to achieve their political purposes, incidents of terrorism surged to historically high levels in the late 1960s and 1970s and became even more frequent in the 1980s. As acts of terrorism spilled outside the boundaries of ongoing conflicts, governments responded to the increased levels of violence by exchanging information about terrorist groups and accumulating intelligence about their membership and activities. Normal police procedures prevented some incidents. Israel, the United States, Great Britain, and Germany went a step farther and formed highly trained and specially equipped counterterrorist units to combat some of the gravest threats. In July 1976 an Israeli Army unit flew to Entebbe, Uganda, and freed a plane full of Jewish hostages. In October 1977, a West German counterterrorist group successfully stormed a Lufthansa aircraft held by terrorists at Mogadishu in Somalia. And in May 1980 members of the British Special Air Service killed six terrorists who had seized twenty-six hostages in the Iranian Embassy in London. While efforts to eradicate terrorism did not yield complete success, the number of incidents seemed to ebb by 1990.

Along with the willingness to use violence against innocent civilians came an erosion of previous restraints on the use of chemicals. The Iraqis used chemicals against the Iranians and compared this use to the use of "pesticides" against "insects." The Soviets also used chemicals in Afghanistan, particularly in the first three years of the war. Additionally, the Egyptians used chemicals in Yemen, the Vietnamese in Kampuchea and Laos, the Libyans in Chad and Northern Uganda, the Cubans in Angola, and the Iraqis against the Kurds. The United States often used riot control gasses and hebicides in Indochina during the Vietnam War. In every case, the use of chemicals occurred in situations in which an opponent lacked adequate means of protection or retaliation. The apparent willingness to employ chemical weapons reflected in part some states' viewing chemical weapons as a "poor man's" nuclear weapon, but it also reflected a widespread willingness to use nearly any means available to achieve victory.

Most major conflicts during the Cold War proved to be protracted rather than brief. The United States hoped to end the Korean War quickly after the landing at Inchon and the breakout from the Pusan perimeter, but the entrance of the Chinese into the war and the complications of political questions and prisoner-of-war issues prevented an early termination of the war. In Vietnam, the Americans had even less success in ending the war early on favorable terms. At the beginning of the Iran-Iraq War, the Iraqi attack against Iran failed despite Iraq's possession of advanced weapons and despite the disorganized state of Iran's forces, and the war dragged on for years. Also, the Russians, despite their numerous advantages and initial success, failed in Afghanistan after years of fighting against a populace determined to pay any price to avoid defeat. Numerous other conflicts, many of which were civil wars stemming from the collapse of colonial empires, tended to last for years. Notable exceptions to long wars occurred with the Israeli victories in 1956, 1967, and 1973, but even these could be considered incidents in a much longer conflict extending over several decades.

In an age of astonishing progress in science and technology, the introduction of advanced weapons and equipment had a particularly significant effect on operations throughout the Cold War. In the Korean War, the combatants used weapons very similar to those of World War II, but in Vietnam the United States fielded a very different force that relied primarily on the helicopter for battlefield mobility. The United States also introduced some rudimentary precision-guided munitions in that war, but the potential of such weapons became most evident in the 1973 Arab-Israeli War. In the Afghanistan War, the Mujahideen used sophisticated and highly mobile air-defense weapons, which relied on advanced electronics, to transform the nature of the fighting. In the last two decades of the Cold War, electronic advances enhanced the ability of commanders to control their forces. With much-improved radios, commanders could maintain better contact with their subordinate units and often had a better grasp of the flow of events. Information about the enemy also increased as the introduction of remarkably capable cameras and high-flying, supersonic aircraft and then satellites permitted the gathering of critical intelligence by the most advanced armed forces. Similarly, advances in computers and information processing permitted improvements in logistical systems. By 1990, the capability of weapons and equipment, as well as intelligence and logistical systems, far exceeded those of 1945.

Despite some significant anomalies, as combat became more lethal, operations became more mobile and linked to air power. Reaching beyond the experience of World War II, battles truly became three-dimensional with the tightening of links between air and ground operations and the introduction of airmobile operations. The Israelis, particularly in the 1967 and 1973 wars, demonstrated their proficiency in conducting lightning-fast campaigns, relying on tightly integrated air and ground forces. Their successes in 1967 and 1973 stemmed more from their superior organizations, strategy, and doctrine than from their superior technology. Advantages in air power and in air mobility, however, did not enable the Americans to overcome the strategic advantages of the North Vietnamese or the tactical mobility of their lightly equipped infantry. Under similar circumstances the Russians failed to overcome the Mujahideen. Iraqi advantages in air power over the Iranians also did not inject mobility into the Iran-Iraq war.

In the final analysis, the conduct of war varied so greatly from conflict to conflict in the Cold War that no single example can serve adequately as a representation of all operations in the era. The key changes in warfare, nevertheless, were both conceptual and technological. Emphasis on limited war reflected the desire of the superpowers to avoid a direct confrontation and escalation to general nuclear war. And the notion of a spectrum of conflict—including low-, mid-, and high-intensity—reflected the various levels of conflict possible prior to all-out nuclear warfare. Within this spectrum, low-intensity conflict—including insurgency, counterinsurgency, and terrorism—received special attention as revolutionary groups often used violence to gain power or achieve their political aims. In an era of remarkable scientific and technological advances, new weapons and equipment frequently appeared, and numerous states fielded modern armed forces equipped with sophisticated arms. The Cold War was thus an era of innovation and change in which military leaders constantly confronted new ideas and weapons, as well as new challenges.

SUGGESTED READINGS

Amstutz, J. Bruce. *Afghanistan: The First Five Years of Soviet Occupation* (Washington, D.C.: National Defense University Press, 1986).

Badri, Hassan el, et al. *The Ramadan War, 1973* (Boulder, Col.: Westview Press, 1977).

Bradsher, Henry S. *Afghanistan and the Soviet Union* (Durham, N.C.: Duke University Press, 1985).

Carver, Michael. *War Since 1945* (London: Ashfield Press, 1990).

Chubin, Shahram, and Charles Tripp. *Iran and Iraq at War* (Boulder, Col.: Westview Press, 1988).

Collins, Joseph H. *The Soviet Invasion of Afghanistan: A Study of the Use of Force in Soviet Foreign Policy* (Lexington, Mass.: Lexington Books, 1986).

Department of National Defence, Canada, Operational Research and Analysis Establishment, ORAE Report No. R 95, G. D. Kaye, D. A. Grant, E. J. Emond. *Major Armed Conflict: A Compendium of Interstate and Intrastate Conflict, 1720 to 1985* (Ottawa, Canada: Orbita Consultants LTD, 1985).

Gawrych, George W. *Key to the Sinai: The Battles for Abu Ageila in the 1956 and 1967 Arab-Israeli Wars* (Fort Leavenworth, Kans.: Combat Studies Institute, 1990).

Hauner, Milan. *The Soviet War in Afghanistan: Patterns of Russian Imperialism* (Philadelphia: Foreign Policy Research Institute, 1991).

Herzog, Chaim. *The Arab-Israeli Wars: War and Peace in the Middle East* (New York: Random House, 1982).

———. *The War of Atonement: October, 1973* (Boston: Little, Brown and Company, 1975).

Hiro, Dilip. *The Longest War: The Iran-Iraq Military Conflict* (New York: Routledge, 1991).

Kahalani, Avigdor. *The Heights of Courage: A Tank Leader's War on the Golan* (Westport, Conn.: Greenwood Press, 1984).

Klass, Rosanne, ed. *Afghanistan: The Great Game Revisited* (New York: Freedom House, 1987).

Laqueur, Walter. *The Age of Terrorism* (Boston: Little, Brown and Company, 1987).

Luttwak, Edward, and Dan Horowitz. *The Israeli Army* (Cambridge, Mass.: Abt Books, 1983).

O'Ballance, Edgar. *No Victor, No Vanquished: The Yom Kippur War* (San Rafael, Calif.: Presidio Press, 1978).

Small, Melvin, and J. David Singer. *Resort to Arms: International and Civil Wars, 1816–1980* (Beverly Hills, Calif.: Sage Publications, 1982).

Thompson, Robert. *War in Peace: Conventional and Guerrilla Warfare Since 1945* (New York: Harmony Books, 1985).

Zabih, Sepehr. *The Iranian Military in Revolution and War* (London: Routledge, 1988).

5

THE AGE OF INTERVENTIONS: PROJECTING POWER AND MAINTAINING PEACE

Interventions in the Cold War

Beyond the Cold War: The Persian Gulf

The United Nations: From Peacekeeping to Peace Enforcement

By the final decade of the Cold War, the major economic and military powers of the West had developed the capability to project force quickly over great distances. Improvements in air and sea transport had enhanced strategic mobility and enabled a few countries to move and support units across thousands of kilometers. In an age of science and technology, these same powers had built arsenals of high-technology weapons with remarkable accuracy and long range. Additionally, advances in electronics and communications permitted more effective command and control of units located at great distances from their homelands. In essence, rapid transport, advanced weapons, and modern communications provided a few countries the capability to project force almost anywhere on the globe. The states possessing this capability—primarily the United States, the Soviet Union, Great Britain, and France—often transported forces during the Cold War to distant regions to protect their own interests, limit the outbreak or spread of violence, or combat aggression. They consequently became embroiled in small conflicts in areas such as the Falklands, Grenada, and Panama.

When the Cold War ended in 1989–1990, the likelihood of interventions did not diminish. Although the confrontation between the two superpowers and their allies disappeared, a more complicated world, split by national, religious, ethnic, and regional differences, appeared. As the constraints of the Cold War dissolved, long-suppressed animosities and aspirations resurfaced, and violence broke out in several regions. Particularly in the Balkans and in the southern part of the former Soviet Union, civil strife, massacres, and pitched battles produced considerable turmoil. Fearing that the violence and turmoil would spread, almost like a cancer, to previously stable regions, some political and military leaders proposed interventions by national and multinational forces to end the violence and restore peace. To most observers' surprise, however, the first major conflict of the post–Cold War era began on August 2, 1990, when Iraq invaded and seized Kuwait. The international community responded to this aggression by transporting massive forces to Southwest Asia and then—in an astounding display of advanced weaponry—destroying much of the Iraqi armed forces with first an aerial attack and then a joint air and ground attack. The swift campaign revealed that not even a relatively wealthy and advanced country like Iraq could match the forces of the major military powers.

The ending of the Cold War also brought changes in the role of the United Nations and its use of intervening forces. No longer constrained by the likelihood of a veto in the U.N. Security Council or by the dangers of a superpower confrontation, U.N. leaders called for "peace-enforcement" operations in which multinational forces would intervene in conflicts, using appropriate levels of force, and restore peace. The reluctance of the United Nations to go beyond providing humanitarian aid in Bosnia-Herzegovina and the difficulties encountered with peace enforcement in Somalia demonstrated the complexities and problems of using international forces in interventions. These conflicts also reminded political and military leaders of the difficulties of employing force in regions riven by strong nationalistic, ethnic, or religious differences.

Interventions in the Cold War

During the Cold War, the major military powers often used their armed forces to support their foreign policy or to achieve specific political objectives. Many of these actions came from the effort to "contain" communism or to prevent a small crisis from erupting into a worldwide conflagration. Actions by the United States, for example, ranged from making a visit to a foreign port with a single warship, to reacting to the seizure of the USS *Pueblo* by the North Koreans in January 1968, to rushing supplies and equipment to Israel in October 1973 during the Arab-Israeli War. About forty crises reached the point where the United States had to confront the possibility of combat.

The U.S. Navy and Marines participated in most of the operations in which Americans were involved. The United States maintained fleets in most major oceans, and the Fleet Marine Force (which was established in

1933) provided battalions of marines that remained afloat with each fleet. In a crisis, marines could move quickly to an area as part of a fleet and could draw upon the fleet's firepower, aviation, and logistical support as they moved ashore. Such forces often proved ideal for dealing with small crises, and other countries such as Great Britain followed the American lead in increasing their fleet's capability to send units ashore.

Following World War II, airborne units and long-distance military air transport provided new means for interventions in distant regions. Much of the increased emphasis on airborne insertions came from the improved range and carrying capacity of military air transport. Particularly in the United States, each new aircraft (such as the Fairchild C-119 Flying Boxcar, the Lockheed C-130 Hercules, the Lockheed C-141B Starlifter, and the Lockheed C-5 Galaxy) provided greater range and carrying capacity than its predecessor. The transition from the C-119, widely used in the Korean War, to the C-5, widely used in the Persian Gulf War, included the change from a cruising speed of 325 kilometers per hour (200 miles per hour) and a range of 1,500 kilometers (900 miles) with a 20,000-pound cargo, to a cruising speed of 830 kilometers per hour (518 miles per hour) and a range of 5,600 kilometers (3,500 miles) with a 170,000-pound cargo. As the capability for air transport of large forces over long distances increased in the mid-to-late 1950s, military leaders recognized that improved transportation enabled light ground units to respond swiftly to an emergency, participate in a small war, or provide initial reinforcements in a much larger war.

An early example of the use of both air- and sea-transported forces occurred in April 1965. In the first American intervention in the Caribbean since U.S. Marines departed from Haiti in 1934, Washington dispatched troops to the Dominican Republic in April 1965. After a revolution broke out in the island nation, President Lyndon B. Johnson, fearing a communist takeover, decided to use military force to restore order. On April 28, 3rd Battalion, 6th Marines flew in helicopters from nearby American ships and landed in Santo Domingo. They assisted in the evacuation of Americans and reinforced the security guard at the U.S. Embassy. After being alerted on the night of April 26, elements of the U.S. Army's 82nd Airborne Division flew on C-130 aircraft from the United States to Puerto Rico and then landed at an airfield near Santo Domingo at 0216 hours on April 30. Members of 7th Special Forces Group and 5th Logistics Command followed. By May 4, more than 17,000 Americans were in Santo Domingo, and by May 17 more than 24,000.

The United States was not the only state to develop the capability for projecting power over great distances. In November 1956, after Gamal Abdel Nasser unexpectedly nationalized the Suez Canal, British and French forces seized the Canal. The operation included French and British airborne battalions jumping onto key targets while British marine battalions came ashore in amphibious landings and heliborne air assaults. Another multinational intervention occurred in November 1964, when U.S. Air Force C-130 aircraft flew 12,000 kilometers from Belgium to the Republic of the Congo and air-dropped a battalion from the Belgian Paracommando Regiment in an attempt to rescue 1,600 European and American hostages. Of those states intervening far outside their own frontiers, France demonstrated a special willingness to intervene in Africa, for it engaged in more than a dozen interventions from 1962 to 1994 in Dakar, Gabon, Chad, Zaire, the Central African Republic, Togo, and Rawanda.

The Falklands

Not all crises had direct ties to the Cold War. When Great Britain responded in 1982 to Argentina's seizure of the Falkland Islands, the roots of the conflict stretched back for more than a century. Known as Las Malvinas in Argentina, the Falklands are an archipelago of some 200 small and two large islands—East Falkland and West Falkland—located about 600 kilometers off the eastern shore of Argentina and 12,000 kilometers from the British Isles. The British claimed sovereignty over the islands, for they had occupied them for more than 150 years and most of the approximately 2,000 inhabitants were of British origin. Argentina denied London's claims and insisted that when Argentina became an independent republic in 1816, it had assumed title to those territories formerly ruled by Spain from Buenos Aires, including the Falklands. As early as 1965, the U.N. General Assembly recognized the dispute between the two states, and for almost two decades the two states discussed the islands' future. In December 1981, however, Argentina began preparing to seize the islands.

On April 2, 1982, the Argentines landed about 1,000 men at Port Stanley on the island of East Falkland and quickly overcame the small Royal Marine detachment. The next day the Argentines seized South Georgia, an island 1,300 kilometers east-southeast of the Falklands and a direct dependency of Britain. They then transported troops and supplies by air and sea until they had about 13,000 troops on the Falkland Islands. British leaders faced the uncomfortable choice of accepting the Argentine action or going to war nearly 12,000 kilometers from Britain with no force organized or prepared for such a contingency, no shore-based air, and little or no knowledge of their enemy.

The importance of sea power for the projection of power over great distances became particularly evident in subsequent British actions. Refusing to accept the Argentine action, the British quickly put together a "retrieval force," the lead elements of which departed Portsmouth on April 5. The task force eventually included a landing force of some 8,000 soldiers and marines and a naval force of more than one hundred ships, including two small aircraft carriers, eight destroyers, fifteen frigates, and six submarines. Fortunately for the British, they had not completed the previously arranged sale of the HMS *Hermes*, a small aircraft carrier, to the Australians. Much of the subsequent campaign would turn on control of the air provided for the British by Vertical/Short Take-off and Landing (VSTOL) aircraft from the HMS *Hermes* and the HMS *Invincible*.

British strategy first sought to isolate the Argentine forces on the Falklands. In early April, London announced that a "maritime" exclusion

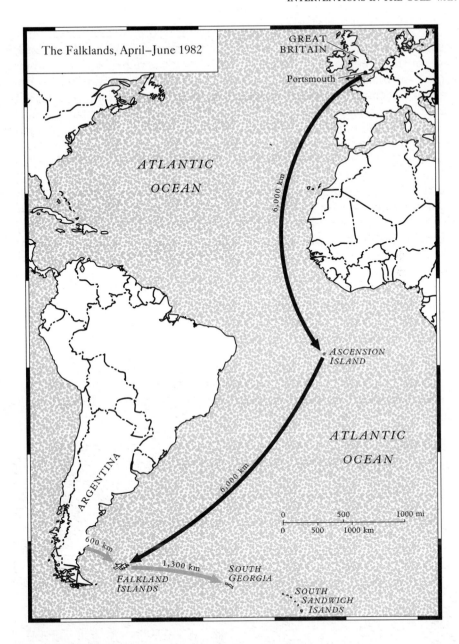

The Falklands, April–June 1982

GREAT BRITAIN

Portsmouth

ATLANTIC OCEAN

6,000 km

ASCENSION ISLAND

ATLANTIC OCEAN

ARGENTINA

6,000 km

600 km

1,300 km

FALKLAND ISLANDS

SOUTH GEORGIA

SOUTH SANDWICH ISANDS

0   500   1000 mi
0   500 1000 km

zone with a 200–nautical mile (370 kilometer) radius would go into effect around the islands on April 12; on April 30 they expanded this into a "total" exclusion zone. Any Argentine aircraft or ship entering this zone would be treated as hostile and could be attacked. On May 1 the British began air and sea bombardment of Port Stanley and Goose Green. The following day, a British nuclear-powered submarine sank the Argentine cruiser, *General Belgrano*, well outside the exclusion zone; 323 members of the Belgrano's crew perished. For the next three weeks the British continued softening up the Argentine defenders on the Falklands.

Meanwhile, the British used Ascension Island, a small air and naval base in the Atlantic midway between Britain and the Falklands, as a staging base for the operation. After hastily assembling the requisite ships and personnel, the main task force, under Rear Admiral John Woodward, sailed from Ascension Island on April 18, even though additional personnel and ships continued to depart Britain for Ascension Island and the Falklands. As the main forces assembled in the South Atlantic, British special operating forces seized South Georgia on April 26, and on May 15 they struck a small Argentine airfield on Pebble Island, just off the north end of West Falkland, and destroyed eleven propeller-driven aircraft.

The Argentines did not remain passive. On May 1, when the British began their attacks on the Falklands, the Argentines launched fifty-six aerial sorties against the enemy's warships. Much to their dismay, they discovered that their best fighters, Mirages and Skyhawks, were no match for British Sea Harriers, which were armed with more advanced AIM-9G Sidewinder heat-seeking missiles. Part of the Argentines' problem came from their keeping their most advanced aircraft at airbases on the continent as many as one thousand kilometers from the Falklands, thus limiting these aircraft to only a few minutes in which they could loiter over a target or engage in a dogfight. In essence, the Argentines could not gain air superiority and could do little more than damage British naval forces and disrupt an amphibious landing. On May 4, from a range of about thirty-five kilometers, however, two Super Etendard aircraft fired two Exocet missiles at British ships; one missed the HMS *Hermes*, but the other struck the HMS *Sheffield*, a destroyer. The

Argentine air force personnel load antipersonnel rockets onto a propeller-driven aircraft. Despite the lethality of such weapons, attacks against British ships came closest to turning the war in Argentina's favor.

British had to abandon the burning *Sheffield*, which had twenty of its crew members killed. Despite the short loiter time, the Argentines continued launching strikes against British warships. On May 25, the Argentines sank the HMS *Coventry* and the *Atlantic Conveyor*, the first with 1,000-pound bombs and the second with an Exocet missile. Throughout the campaign, courageous Argentine pilots would sink six British ships and damage eighteen others. Had they possessed more than five of the French-manufactured Exocet missiles, they might have inflicted even greater damage.

By mid-May, the British had advanced into the South Atlantic, isolated Argentine forces on the Falklands, recaptured South Georgia, and launched commando raids and aerial reconnaissance in preparation for an amphibious landing. At dawn on May 21, after a diversionary operation farther south, British forces began landing at Port San Carlos and San Carlos on the northwest corner of East Falkland. The landing of the 3rd Commando Brigade (a marine unit commanded by Brigadier Julian Thompson) and two parachute battalions went smoothly and met almost no opposition, but Argentine pilots braved heavy antiaircraft fire to strike British ships. The British intended to consolidate their beachhead, unload supplies, and advance only a short distance until the 5th Infantry Brigade arrived. Although under heavy aerial attack, the British unloaded 12,000 tons of cargo in the first five days.

Concerned about British losses and desiring to show greater progress, London ordered the capture of Darwin and Goose Green, twenty kilometers south of the beachhead. Advancing on the night of May 27, the

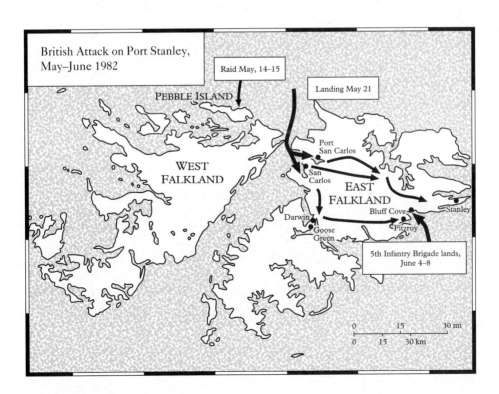

British Attack on Port Stanley, May–June 1982

Raid May, 14–15

Landing May 21

PEBBLE ISLAND

WEST FALKLAND

Port San Carlos

San Carlos

EAST FALKLAND

Darwin

Goose Green

Bluff Cove

Fitzroy

Stanley

5th Infantry Brigade lands, June 4–8

0   15   30 mi

0   15   30 km

2nd Battalion of the Parachute Regiment attacked early on May 28 and encountered strong opposition. Though their battalion commander was killed, the British continued pressing the Argentine defenders until they offered to surrender. Much to the paratroopers' surprise, more than 1,200 Argentines, some of whom were from the air force, surrendered their weapons and marched into captivity. With little support, a single British battalion had defeated a force triple its own strength.

The battle, however, produced considerable strain between the British military and the news media. Shortly before the attack on Goose Green, the BBC World News Service announced the location and mission of the 2nd Battalion. Other difficulties stemmed from few of the reporters having a sophisticated understanding of military affairs, and fewer still being prepared for the rigors of marching across the Falklands. Some reporters in the South Atlantic became particularly angry when they realized that their reports were being heavily censored and that some of the information removed by censors in the South Atlantic was being released by the Ministry of Defence in London.

After Goose Green, the British turned their attention to the capture of Port Stanley on the opposite side of East Falkland. Located at the tip of a twenty-five kilometer peninsula, Port Stanley had three chains of mountains between it and the approaching enemy. The Argentine commander, Brigadier General Mario B. Menéndez, had about 9,000 troops and placed them in well-organized and strong defensive positions in these mountains. Though apprehensive about an amphibious landing near Port Stanley, he evidently thought these mountainous positions were impregnable, and he expected his defenses and the approaching winter to force the British to seek a diplomatic end to the war. His lack of confidence in his soldiers, mostly conscripts, and the absence of air and sea support convinced him to wage a passive campaign and to keep his forces in static defenses. The morale of the defenders was very low. Few had proper cold-weather clothing, and many suffered from inadequate rations. Most apparently felt abandoned.

For the assault on Port Stanley, the British had intended to transport their troops by helicopter, but the sinking of the *Atlantic Conveyor*, a container ship, had resulted in the loss of critical helicopter support. Consequently many soldiers and marines had to trudge across some eighty kilometers of cold, wet, difficult terrain. The British advanced on two routes, one along the northern coast of East Falkland and the other along the southern coast. On June 1 they used helicopters to land troops on two mountains in the most westward chain, and other forces arrived by foot a few days later. On June 5 a battalion from the 5th Infantry Brigade landed on the coast to the south of the 3rd Commando Brigade, and two later days, another battalion landed but suffered heavily from an Argentine air strike.

The British land-force commander, Major General Jeremy Moore, eventually had two brigades in place for the final assault on Port Stanley. After doing everything possible to convince the Argentines to surrender, he decided to make a night attack on a broad front. On the night of June 11–12, the 3rd Commando Brigade, reinforced by the 3rd Parachute Battalion, attacked with three battalions abreast and seized, after some difficult

British troops rappelling from a helicopter. The superb training and highly competent performance of British troops enabled them easily to defeat the poorly trained and unmotivated Argentines.

fighting, the second chain of mountains. Two nights later the 5th Brigade passed through the marines and attacked the third chain. The British battalion in the north encountered strong opposition, but the two battalions in the south met little resistance. The Argentine defenders struck the northern battalion in two minor counterattacks, but heavy fire broke them. The failure of these counterattacks left the British in command of high ground from which they could dominate all the open ground to the west of Stanley. Within minutes, Argentine defenses collapsed. As the defenders fled in panic toward Port Stanley, white flags appeared throughout the Argentine positions. At 2100 hours on June 14, Menéndez signed an "instrument of surrender" given him by Moore.

In a stormy, mountainous, freezing environment, the British had won a difficult campaign. They had defeated a numerically superior force and had overcome the significant logistical problem of transporting and supporting large forces 12,000 kilometers from their home base. The war demonstrated the strengths of a well-trained, prepared force. British soldiers and marines, all of whom were volunteers, performed much better than the Argentines, most of whom were conscripts. Only the Argentine pilots performed on a par with the British. The war also demonstrated the importance of joint operations. Unlike the Argentines, who encountered problems in getting their services to cooperate, the British military achieved excellent cooperation among air, land, and sea elements as they waged a relatively short-warning, intense operation against an unexpected adversary. Another significant feature of the war was the demonstrated effect of the high-technology weapons entering the world's arsenals in the 1980s. The lethality and effectiveness of the Exocet over great distances cost the British dearly, just as the technical advantages of the more advanced Sidewinder missile cost the Argentines dearly. In the final analysis, however, the British won because of their ability to project power over great distances and their mastery of basic military skills.

Operation "Urgent Fury" in Grenada

Another significant intervention during the Cold War occurred in October 1983 when the United States relied on air and sea transport to intervene on extremely short notice in Grenada, a small island in the Caribbean. With marine units relying on naval transport, and army units relying on air transport, the brief conflict turned out to be unexpectedly difficult because of limited planning time, the great distances involved, the variety of forces participating, and the lack of adequate intelligence. Around noon on Saturday, October 22, President Reagan ordered the intervention in Grenada. Because of the breakdown of order on the island, he was initially concerned with the safety of Americans, but he soon expanded the operation's objectives to include restoring democratic government in Grenada and eliminating current and future Cuban intervention on the island. The Cubans were building a major air base in Grenada, and he feared the spread of Cuban and communist influence in the Caribbean.

A military policeman guards prisoners in Grenada. Planning for Urgent Fury included preparation not only for transport and combat but also for logistical support, medical care, civil affairs, and a host of other requirements.

The Joint Chiefs of Staff issued the formal order around 1700 hours on Saturday for Operation "Urgent Fury." Anticipating a mission to ensure the safety of Americans, the Commander-in-Chief of the Atlantic Command (CINCLANT) had already organized a joint force (designated Joint Task Force 120, under the command of Vice Admiral Joseph Metcalf, III) and sent it toward Grenada. Subsequent intelligence estimates of enemy forces in Grenada, however, identified about 700 Cubans (of whom 25 percent were military), 1,200–1,500 members of the People's Revolutionary Army (PRA), and 2,000–5,000 members of the People's Revolutionary Militia (PRM). Though the figures turned out to be inflated, the opposition appeared to consist of about ten combat battalions, plus supporting units. Responding to broader goals and facing what they thought was a large enemy force, planners increased the size of the American force by adding army units, flown in by the air force, to the operation. What had initially been envisaged as a relatively small and simple navy-marine rescue of American students became a much larger and more complicated operation.

Located about 200 kilometers off the coast of Venezuela, the island of Grenada is shaped like an oval, about thirty kilometers long and twelve kilometers wide, with a broad peninsula jutting out from the southwest corner. Much of the island consists of mountainous jungle, surrounded by a narrow coastal plain on which most of the island's towns are located. The Point Salines airfield with a 3,000-meter runway is on the peninsula in the southwest corner, and the capital city of St. George's is about seven kilometers north on the west coast of the island. Farther to the north and near the

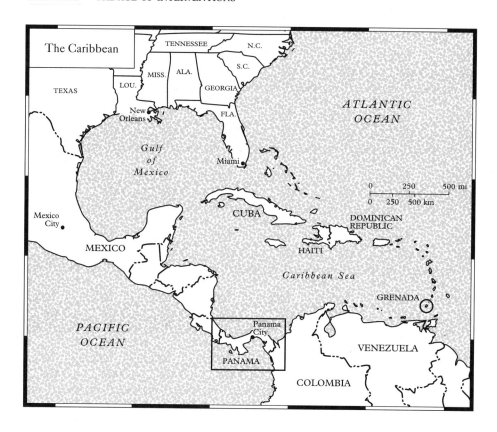

The Caribbean

ATLANTIC OCEAN

TENNESSEE   N.C.

S.C.

MISS.   ALA.

TEXAS   LOU.   GEORGIA

New Orleans   FLA.

Gulf of Mexico   Miami

Mexico City   CUBA   DOMINICAN REPUBLIC

MEXICO   HAITI

Caribbean Sea

GRENADA

PACIFIC OCEAN   Panama City

PANAMA   VENEZUELA

COLOMBIA

0   250   500 mi

0   250   500 km

east coast is Pearls Airport. The airfields at Point Salines and Pearls and the city of St. George's became the focal points of American efforts. As planning proceeded, marine units received responsibility for the northern part of the island and army units for the southern part. Except for two small areas north and south of St. George's, the beaches were rocky, blocked by reefs, and unsuitable for amphibious landings.

The first force to move toward Grenada was an amphibious task force that—as a precaution—had been ordered around midnight on October 20 by CINCLANT to sail toward Grenada. The task force included the navy's Amphibious Squadron Four, consisting of five ships, and the 22nd Marine Amphibious Unit, consisting of an infantry battalion and a medium helicopter squadron. When the intervention began, however, Special Operations Forces led the Americans into Grenada. Among those participating were Delta Force, Seal Team 6, and C Company, 1st Battalion, 75th Rangers. The first attempt to use Special Operations Forces miscarried on Sunday night, October 23–24, when a joint Seal–air force combat-control team failed to land on Grenada and set up a sophisticated navigational aid for incoming aircraft. Early on Tuesday, October 25, other forces failed to seize the radio transmitting station north of St. George's and to release political prisoners from Richmond Hill Prison. A Seal team managed to seize the transmitting tower, but a counterattack by PRA soldiers forced them to withdraw. Nonetheless, the Seals destroyed the tower and prevented the PRA from transmitting any warning to the militia. In the one notable success of Special Operations Forces, a Seal team landed in helicopters at the Government House just outside St. George's and secured the safety of the British Governor General, Sir Paul Scoon. Despite strong counterattacks from PRA soldiers using Soviet armored personnel carriers, the Seals retained control over the Government House until rescued by marines the following morning.

Marine and army landings followed the actions of the Special Operations forces. Around 0730 hours on Tuesday, after receiving only a few small bursts of automatic weapons fire, heliborne marines secured Pearls Airport in the northeast corner of Grenada. Shortly thereafter, helicopters landed a company on a soccer field in the center of the town of Grenville about two kilometers to the south of Pearls Airport. The marines encountered no opposition and quickly secured the town and its port without taking any casualties. Farther to the south, U.S. Army units encountered much stronger opposition against well-prepared defenders. The first soldiers to arrive were from 1st Battalion, 75th Rangers; they had the mission of securing the Point Salines airfield before the arrival of 82nd Airborne Division. Not knowing whether they would land on the airfield or make an airborne drop, they flew about 3,000 kilometers from Savannah, Georgia, on C-130 aircraft. After the lead aircraft encountered strong antiaircraft fire, the ranger battalion commander ordered his soldiers to jump from 500 feet, thereby limiting their exposure to enemy fire. When the rangers landed around the airfield at 0530 hours on Tuesday, they received heavy automatic weapons and mortar fire from defenders on the high ground to the north of the airfield, but they quickly secured the airfield's periphery and cleared the runway of construction equipment, wire barriers, and metal stakes. Around 0900 hours, the rangers rescued 138 medical students at the True Blue campus just off the eastern end of the airfield.

While the rangers fought to expand the area under their control around the Point Salines airfield, the first elements of 82nd Airborne Division departed Fort Bragg, North Carolina, shortly after 1000 hours and landed at Point Salines around 1400 hours. Like the rangers, they had traveled more than 3,000 kilometers. When the first battalion from the 82nd landed, accompanied by the division commander, Major General Edward Trobaugh, sniper and automatic weapons fire continued sporadically from the high ground around the airfield. Despite the importance of pushing on to St. George's, Trobaugh focused on protecting the airfield and awaiting the arrival of another battalion before moving into the steep, heavily forested terrain along the route to Grenada's capital. Troop strength at Point Salines increased slowly because the unfinished runway had insufficient ramp space for parking landed aircraft, and a huge backlog of incoming forces and equipment quickly developed. The second battalion did not arrive until around 0300 hours on Wednesday.

On Tuesday afternoon, Admiral Metcalf decided to bypass the Cuban and PRA defenders around Point Salines and land marines at St.

George's. Around 1830 hours, without encountering any opposition, thirteen amphibian tracks landed about two kilometers north of St. George's. Using utility landing craft, a platoon of M-60 tanks and jeeps with heavy machine guns and antitank weapons followed. The next morning, around 0730 hours, one of the marine companies and the tank platoon reached the house where PRA soldiers besieged the Seals and Sir Paul Scoon. The appearance of the tanks and amphibian vehicles dispersed the PRA forces. On that day and the next, against little more than sniper fire, the marines secured the harbor works and the hilltops around St. George's.

At 0630 hours on Wednesday, two battalions of infantry from the 82nd Division attacked northeast out of the Point Salines airfield into the Calliste barracks, killing sixteen and capturing eighty-six Cubans. They then climbed a steep hill north of Calliste and captured a large ammunition depot about one and a half kilometers to the northeast. Six huge warehouses contained weapons, ammunition, uniforms, spare parts, and vehicles. As the paratroopers advanced, the rangers used marine CH-46s and CH-53s to travel to Grande Anse (about two kilometers to the north of the Point Salines airfield) and rescue additional students there. Despite the objections of one marine commander, who initially refused to transport army troops on marine helicopters, the rangers landed at about 1615 hours and quickly evacuated 224 students.

On Thursday, October 27, the 82nd, with six battalions on the ground plus its divisional artillery, pushed north toward St. George's. The operation went smoothly except for a navy A-7 aircraft accidentally strafing the headquarters of the 2nd Brigade and wounding sixteen soldiers, one of whom later died. At 1630 hours, the rangers launched an air assault into Calivigny Barracks, about five kilometers east of the Salines airfield. Though the rangers encountered no enemy, two helicopters collided, killing and injuring about two dozen men. The securing of the barracks around 2100 hours marked the end of significant military activity in Grenada.

Despite overwhelming superiority, the Americans had encountered many difficulties. Some problems stemmed from the operation's being cobbled together hastily without the participants having the time or opportunity for coordination. Other difficulties, particularly for the army and air force, revolved around the long distance—about 3,000 kilometers—between the units' home stations and Grenada. The complexities of launching an operation over such a long distance were accentuated by confusion over questions of command and control and by the lack of direct radio communications between the 82d Airborne, the marines, and Admiral Metcalf. As with many combat operations, intelligence could have been more accurate and timely. Urgent Fury became a controversial operation with criticisms surfacing for most aspects of the operation but focusing on the inability of the services to work together smoothly.

The October 1983 intervention in Grenada also marked a low point in relations between the U.S. armed forces and the news media. Heeding Department of Defense requests, President Reagan placed a total ban on press coverage during the first two days of the invasion and maintained tight restrictions on reporting in the following week. The Department of Defense provided several reasons for maintaining tight control over news reporting, including the necessity for secrecy and the inability to provide security for reporters. Some critics charged, however, that the American military leaders were suspicious of reporters and wanted to avoid negative media coverage. In the final analysis, strained relations between the military and the news media heightened criticism of the operation.

Operation "Just Cause" in Panama

Over the next few years the United States made some improvements in its conduct of joint operations and rapid interventions, and the effect of these changes was obvious in December 1989 when U.S. forces seized control of Panama. For several years tension had increased between Washington and Panama, and on Friday, December 15, the Panamanian National Assembly gave sweeping powers to General Manuel A. Noriega and declared Panama in a "state of war" against the United States as long as American "aggression" continued. On Sunday, December 17, President George Bush ordered U.S. military forces to intervene in Panama. In an address from the White House on the day of the operation, he explained that the objectives of "Just Cause" were "to safeguard the lives of Americans, to defend democracy in Panama, to combat drug trafficking, and to protect the integrity of the Panama Canal Treaty."

Unlike Urgent Fury in Grenada, Just Cause was smoothly and almost flawlessly executed. Those planning the operation relied on existing command relationships; they also had the crucial advantage of having sufficient time for planning and preparation and having 13,000 troops and a U.S.-controlled airbase immediately available. These advantages enabled most of the participating units to be well rehearsed for their combat mission and thoroughly familiar with the terrain. Even those units that parachuted onto key targets after being flown from the United States in transport planes had detailed information about their objectives. By striking twenty-seven targets almost simultaneously in the night, the Americans quickly gained control of Panama. Within seven hours after the assault began, the Panamanian Defense Forces no longer existed as a cohesive military organization and offered no organized resistance against U.S. forces.

Thus in the final decade of the Cold War, improvements in the ability to project force from fleets and increases in the cruising range and payloads of military air transport enhanced the capabilities of a few countries to intervene quickly in distant regions. Because of the need for rapid action over long distances, accomplishing critical planning and establishing effective command arrangements remained difficult. Problems with intelligence, logistics, communications, and coordination also appeared frequently. Interventions, nevertheless, continued to rely on offensive action and sought to overwhelm more poorly equipped and trained opponents swiftly.

Beyond the Cold War:
The Persian Gulf

As the Cold War ended, political and military leaders recognized the dangers of aggression from rogue states seeking territory, influence, or advantages. Common sense underlined the need to react swiftly with relatively large forces to counter such aggression. Hardly anyone, however, expected a major conflict immediately after the end of the Cold War. In many ways, the Persian Gulf War was as much a surprise as the Korean War, but unlike that experience, the United States, whose forces carried most of the weight of the war, proved to be far better prepared. Unfortunately for the Iraqis, the United States had developed the capability to reinforce Europe by transporting forces over great distances rapidly, and the campaign in Southwest Asia proved to be ideal for forces and doctrine designed to fight the Soviets in central Europe.

The war began when the military forces of President Saddam Hussein of Iraq invaded the tiny desert sheikdom of Kuwait on August 2, 1990. In a bold operation, Iraqi forces seized control of Kuwait's capital city and its rich oil fields and drove the emir of Kuwait into exile. With only 20,000 troops, thirty-six combat aircraft, and 275 tanks, Kuwait was no match for the Iraqis. Iraq's aggression and quick success convinced the international community that it threatened the traditional balance of power in the Middle East and Southwest Asia. Led by Egypt, Arab governments in the region sought an "Arab solution" to ease Iraq out of Kuwait, but Iraq announced on August 8 the annexation of Kuwait, dashing any hopes for peaceful resolution of the crisis. At a meeting of the Arab League shortly after the invasion, twelve of the twenty-one members expressed support for a United Nations embargo against Iraq and endorsed Saudi Arabia's invitation to the United States to send troops to deter Iraqi aggression. They also agreed to send Arab forces to defend Saudi Arabia. Many Arabs recognized that Saddam's ambitious desire to establish Iraq as the dominant power in the Middle East threatened their own way of life.

The seizure of Kuwait also captured the attention of much of the world. With the Soviet Union in disarray, with the Warsaw Pact crumbling, and with the two Germanys about to be reunited, the world seemed to be entering a period of peace. In what many hoped would be a new world order, aggression by one state against another could not be tolerated. For many, Saddam seemed to be nothing more than a "terrorist with an army." Moreover, Saddam's belligerence jeopardized much of the world's oil supplies. By seizing Kuwait and declaring it the nineteenth province of Iraq, Saddam doubled Iraq's oil reserves and gained control over 20 percent of the world's proven reserves. Even worse, his position in the Gulf, if unchallenged, could eventually allow him to dominate Saudi Arabia and increase his control to 40 percent of the world's oil reserves. The oil-dependent nations of the world could tolerate neither Iraq's aggression nor the threat of its controlling the world's oil supplies.

King Fahd of Saudi Arabia and General H. Norman Schwarzkopf. Keeping the diverse coalition together proved to be one of the most complex challenges of the war.

Much of the world united against Saddam. In a very important change closely associated with the ending of the Cold War and the willingness of Russia to oppose the Iraqi action, the United Nations Security Council adopted a resolution condemning the Iraqi invasion of Kuwait and soon imposed mandatory sanctions and an embargo against Iraq. After the United Nations adopted a resolution authorizing the use of force, thirty-six countries—not including Kuwait—dispatched forces to the Gulf.

Particularly during the period when the coalition was rushing ground forces to Saudi Arabia, the Iraqi ground forces, which had recently emerged from an eight-year war against Iran, seemed large and capable. Iraq's army dwarfed not only the other armies in the area—except for Iran's—but also many of those in Europe. As the fourth largest army in the world, it was bigger than those of Britain and France combined. It also possessed huge quantities of modern equipment and seemed to have a formidable tank force. U.S. intelligence agencies estimated that the Iraqis had some 4,550 main battle tanks and 2,880 armored personnel carriers in and around Kuwait. Though the great majority of the Iraqi tanks were older Soviet T-54 and T-62 models, about 500 of the main battle tanks were Soviet T-72 tanks, which weighed about 45 tons and were considered among the best tanks in the world. As for artillery, the Iraqis had 3,257 pieces in or near Kuwait; some analysts credited the Iraqis with a 7-to-1 advantage in artillery. The Iraqi air force had about 950 combat aircraft, and with more than 4,000 air defense guns and 300 long-range, Soviet-made SA-2 and SA-4 ground-to-air missiles, Iraqi air defenses seemed formidable.

Moreover, Saddam possessed a substantial store of chemical weapons and during the Iran-Iraq War had demonstrated his willingness to use them. The only thing lacking in Saddam's arsenal was nuclear weapons, but evidence strongly suggested that he was making a concerted effort to develop such weapons. On August 21, Pentagon officials acknowledged that the Iraqis had moved medium-range ballistic missiles into Kuwait. The missiles were Scud missiles which could carry conventional high-explosive warheads or chemical warheads with mustard or nerve gas. The possibility of Scud missiles spewing chemical or biological agents against coalition soldiers or against unprotected civilians caused considerable concern.

American Forces in the Gulf

The coalition facing Iraq established a centralized command system for Arab and Western air forces, but no single commander controlled all the coalition's ground forces. The coalition had two parallel commands for ground forces, one Arab and the other Western. A Saudi Arabian general officer maintained relatively loose command over the various Arab ground units. The Commander-in-Chief of U.S. Central Command, General H. Norman Schwarzkopf, commanded all American forces in the region of the Persian Gulf and Southwest Asia; the French and British governments also gave him control of their ground forces. As for air forces, U.S. Lieutenant General Charles A. Horner acted as the coalition's air commander and worked directly under Schwarzkopf.

Of those nations sending forces, the largest number by far came from the United States. With lead elements arriving on August 8, the 82nd Airborne Division was the first large American ground unit to arrive, followed by U.S. Marines. Virtually all of the first 35,000 American troops in Saudi Arabia were flown there by about sixty commercial aircraft chartered by the U.S. military, but the bulk of their equipment came by sea and arrived weeks later. When it became apparent that the U.N. embargo would not force the Iraqis to withdraw, the Americans increased their offensive capability. In November, President George Bush announced that the United States would substantially increase the size of its ground forces in Saudi Arabia by mobilizing additional reserve forces and by moving U.S. Army units from Europe. Shortly thereafter, armored units from the U.S. Army began to arrive.

The move of VII Corps from Germany was particularly challenging. After the public announcement on November 8 of VII Corps' deployment to Southwest Asia, the Americans moved 122,000 soldiers and 40,000 major pieces of equipment to the air- and seaports of embarkation, using 465 trains, 312 barges, and 119 convoys. From these ports, the corps used 578 aircraft and 140 ships to travel to Saudi Arabia. After arriving at ports in Saudi Arabia, some VII Corps units traveled as far as 500 kilometers in convoys along Saudi highways. Though the entire move took about twelve weeks, most tactical units arrived in sufficient time to conduct training in the desert in chemical protection, weapons firing, land navigation, breaching procedures, and tactical operations.

The Americans brought with them the technological weapons that they had created during the 1970s and 1980s. The air force's F-117A Stealth bomber was invisible to Iraqi defenses throughout the war. Precision-guided munitions from the F-117A and other aircraft allowed them to attack targets with unheard-of accuracy. Air-launched and sea-launched cruise missiles could strike targets from extreme distances and with accuracy similar to precision-guided munitions. Electronic warfare aircraft could jam and distort enemy radars, while air-launched missiles sought and destroyed active radars. The army also possessed weapons that allowed its troops to seek out and kill its opponents at great distances. Infrared and other devices allowed U.S. ground forces to "see" at night, while their opponents remained blinded by the darkness. Additionally, the Americans' training, doctrine, and operational conceptions provided them significant advantages. The competence, initiative, and flexibility of U.S. air and ground forces rendered irrelevant all considerations of Iraqi numbers, quality equipment, and battle experience.

From the beginning, it was clear that women would play a larger role in this war than any in history. Of the more than half-million American personnel in the Persian Gulf region at the height of the war, 35,000 were women. They operated air-defense systems, made intelligence assessments, drove trucks, sorted mail, operated water purification units, repaired equipment, acted as military police, and performed a host of other functions. Women helicopter pilots flew in combat zones, but not on direct combat missions; they moved supplies and soldiers around the battlefield and evacuated wounded soldiers. When the fighting began, five women were killed in hostile action; two others were captured by the Iraqis, one when her truck became lost and the other when her helicopter crashed.

Planning the Coalition's Defense and Attack

The outbreak of the war caught American military and diplomatic planners by surprise. Much of the prewar planning had viewed the Persian Gulf region as secondary to the European theater. Intelligence assessments in the region had focused mainly on the possibility of a Soviet advance, not on an Iraqi attack through Kuwait into Saudi Arabia. For most of August, as the

U.S. military deployed forces over enormous distances, the possibility of Iraq's moving south caused grave concern, but the situation was not as serious as it appeared at the time. While the Iraqis threatened Saudi Arabia, they possessed neither the training nor the logistical capabilities that such an operation would have required. By the end of August the Iraqis had settled into defensive positions in Kuwait to wait out the gathering coalition. Because of the solid performance of Iraqi defenses during the eight-year Iran-Iraq War, coalition commanders expected these positions to be strong.

The rapid buildup of U.S. combat aircraft initially focused General Schwarzkopf's attention on the use of air power. Six days after Iraq invaded Kuwait, he asked the air staff in Washington to prepare plans for aerial attacks against the Iraqis. Within a few days, a planning cell in the Pentagon produced a plan called "Instant Thunder" which envisaged a massive strategic air campaign against Iraq. Air planners believed that such a campaign would prevent a costly ground war and in six to nine days could achieve American national objectives, including "the immediate, complete, and unconditional withdrawal of all Iraqi forces from Kuwait." Schwarzkopf accepted the plan on August 10, apparently viewing it as a retaliatory plan. After briefing General Colin Powell, Chairman of the Joint Chiefs of Staff, planners added another phase to Instant Thunder, entitled "An Operational Air Campaign Against Iraqi Forces in Kuwait," which focused on destroying the Iraqi army. The air planners believed that Schwarzkopf intended to use only air power to force the Iraqis from Kuwait.

As events unfolded, however, Schwarzkopf conceived of the campaign against Iraq in four phases. In phase I, air attacks would strike Iraq. In phase II, coalition aircraft would gain air superiority over Kuwait. In phase III, air attacks would reduce Iraqi ground forces and destroy their ability to use chemicals. And in phase IV, ground forces with support from air forces would eject Iraqi forces from Kuwait. Schwarzkopf also made the crucial decision that Horner would run the air war and that the other air forces (marine and navy, but not army), as well as the other coalition air forces, would come under Horner's command. That decision allowed air planners to develop an integrated approach to air attacks against Iraq. To blend Instant Thunder into overall aerial planning, Horner established a special planning group in Saudi Arabia. The name Instant Thunder was dropped, and the air attack against Iraq—in essence a strategic campaign—became "Offensive Campaign Phase I." Before the first air attacks began, however, the idea of the air war being divided into distinct phases had almost disappeared, and target lists for phases I, II, and III had merged. Planners expected the focus of the aerial attacks to shift gradually from the strategic to the tactical arena and from Iraq to Kuwait.

Initial plans for the ground forces emphasized the defense, but early in September, Schwarzkopf's staff began planning for an offensive. On October 6, planners presented several alternatives to Schwarzkopf who selected an option calling for a two-week air attack followed by a ground attack that would penetrate Iraqi forces and advance into southern Kuwait. With the coalition's ground forces clearly outnumbered, planners ruled out a bold envelopment of the Iraqi forces. Concerned about the possibility of heavy casualties in such an attack, Schwarzkopf directed his staff on October 15 to begin planning for an attack with larger ground forces. His staff immediately began developing plans for an attack through the great Iraqi desert and around the flank of the Iraqis in Kuwait. In late October, Schwarzkopf approved the concept for an envelopment of Iraqi forces, and in mid-November, with President Bush having announced the commitment of VII Corps, he set mid-January as the time for the offensive.

The Coalition's Aerial Attack

Almost from the beginning of the crisis, the coalition had a distinct advantage in air power, concentrating 2,614 aircraft in the Persian Gulf area, 1,990 of which were American. Shortly before 0300 hours (local time) on January 17, 1991, the coalition's air plan unfolded when army AH-64 Apache helicopters attacked several frontier early-warning radar sites. The destruction of those sites created a corridor through which F-15Es were able to strike at Scud missile bases in western Iraq. A few minutes later, F-117A Stealth aircraft, undetected by Iraqi radar, arrived over Baghdad and other targets and began dropping precision-guided munitions. Minutes later, a wave of "Tomahawk" cruise missiles from naval vessels in the Gulf slammed into targets throughout Baghdad and elsewhere. At the same time, air-launched cruise missiles from B-52G bombers, which had flown from air bases as distant as Louisiana, hit their targets. The strikes caught the Iraqis completely by surprise, because they possessed no means of detecting the inward-bound missiles or Stealth aircraft.

The coalition made the destruction of the Iraqis' air defenses a high priority. From carriers in the Red Sea, the U.S. Navy sent F/A-18 Hornets and EA-6B Prowlers to strike Baghdad from the west; at the same time U.S. Air Force F-4G Wild Weasels approached the capital from the south. Decoys and drones gave the impression of even larger attacking groups, and chaff created additional confusion. As the Iraqi radar sites tracked the incoming aircraft, antiradar missiles homed in on their radar signals. Following this attack, many Iraqi air-defense units turned off their radar and fired their weapons aimlessly into the sky. Within hours, the Iraqi air-defense system ceased to operate as a coherent, functioning military system. Few Iraqi aircraft rose to meet the tide of aircraft sweeping over Saddam's lands; the few that did soon disappeared in explosions of air-to-air missiles.

When dawn came, amazed coalition air commanders discovered that they had lost only one aircraft during the night—far less than their prewar expectations of twenty-five to fifty aircraft. Most important, coalition air forces had achieved air supremacy over Iraq. Since coalition aircraft at heights above 10,000 feet could operate beyond the effective range of enemy antiaircraft guns, subsequent attacks suffered only minimal casualties. The coalition now had the luxury of continuing air attacks almost indefinitely.

The first night, coalition aircraft and missiles also hit a large number of special sites, particularly the nuclear, chemical, and biological special weapons programs on which the Iraqi regime was hard at work. Other strikes destroyed command-and-control centers, communications networks, and enemy airfields. Planners targeted Iraq's electrical network particularly heavily; they believed its destruction would lead to the collapse of communications, make it more difficult for the Iraqi military to function, and perhaps even lead to a collapse of national morale. By dawn on the morning of January 17, Iraq was well on its way to defeat.

Continuing the Air Attacks

From the allied perspective, the first few days of the air attack went like clockwork. Not only were losses well below expectations, but electrical power systems were down throughout much of Iraq. On day three weather began to interfere with air operations. Throughout the rest of the war, weather conditions created numerous difficulties for those planning and conducting air operations. Whatever the difficulties, the volume and accuracy of air attacks wore down the Iraqi military. At the end of the first week of air attacks, F-111Fs and the F-117As went after hardened shelters on Iraqi airbases. These attacks destroyed a substantial number of shelters on enemy airfields, as well as the aircraft parked inside. In a desperate move, Saddam

A Patriot missile leaps from its launcher. Initially designed to engage aircraft, the Patriot became the first successful antimissile system after modifications were made to the missile and its computers. Before the war its antimissile capability had undergone only limited testing.

ordered many of his remaining aircraft to fly to Iran. This action eliminated the Iraqi air force as a military factor in the war.

Despite the intensity of the coalition's air strikes, the Iraqis managed, beginning on January 18, to launch ninety-three Scud missiles, most of which were aimed at population centers in Saudi Arabia and Israel. Though lacking accuracy, the Scuds posed a strategic threat, for Saddam expected Scud attacks on Israel to bring Israeli forces into the war and thereby shatter the coalition. The U.S. Army's Patriot air-defense system intercepted 70 percent of the Scud missiles fired at Saudi Arabia and 40 percent of those fired at Israel. These were the first missiles ever intercepted in combat by an antimissile system, and the civilians and soldiers who had been the targets of Scud missiles loudly applauded the success of the Patriot. Nonetheless, the performance of the Patriot missiles was not flawless. Since the Patriot had been designed to explode near an incoming missile, not necessarily to destroy the warhead, some of the Scuds intercepted by the Patriots still caused damage on the ground. Due to a problem with computer software, a Patriot battery north of Dhahran failed to detect an incoming Scud missile on February 25, and the missile hit a barracks, killing twenty-eight American soldiers and wounding ninety-seven others.

On January 29, the Iraqis launched a raid with the 5th Mechanized Division, plus elements of two other divisions. They recognized that air attacks would continue for the foreseeable future. Moreover, air attacks had entirely shut down the Iraqi capacity to acquire intelligence. Consequently, they hoped the raid could gain valuable intelligence and perhaps force the coalition to begin the ground attack. Although the Iraqis got some troops into the Saudi frontier town of Khafji, most of the raiding force did not achieve even a brief success. One of the armored brigades got stuck in a minefield where coalition aircraft massacred vehicles and troops alike. Aircraft also hit units that were supposed to support the attack on Khafji and prevented them from reaching the front lines. By the end of the Khafji battle, the Iraqis had suffered several thousand casualties and lost several hundred armored vehicles. Khafji made clear that the Iraqis could not concentrate their armored and mechanized forces under a sky—night or day—dominated by coalition aircraft.

Air attacks thoroughly disrupted Iraq's command-and-control systems, political as well as military. Over the night of February 12–13, F117As executed a series of particularly heavy raids against Iraqi headquarters and bunker targets in the Baghdad area. One of those targets was the al-Firdos bunker; intelligence indicated that the Iraqis had just activated the bunker. Unfortunately, no one in either intelligence or in the planning cycle knew that the bunker also served as a shelter for families of the governmental elite (Saddam's regime constructed no bunkers for the general population of Baghdad). The result was a tragic loss of civilian lives that television immediately broadcast to the world. In response, political authorities in the United States forbade further attacks on Baghdad without Washington's approval; attacks on Iraq's political infrastructure virtually halted. Late in the war, F-117As did strike a few targets in Baghdad, but none that carried the risk of further civilian casualties.

As the time for the ground attack approached, coalition aircraft struck operational-level targets such as Iraq's military supply lines to Kuwait and the Republican Guard divisions in northern Kuwait. Among their targets, they destroyed thirty-one railway and highway bridges and thirty-two pontoon bridges. They also destroyed important fuel- and lubricant-distribution centers. At the end of the first week in February, the focus of the air campaign moved to preparing the battlefield for the ground attack.

Early in February, F-111F pilots discovered that their infrared sensors could accurately spot armored and other vehicles in the desert because of the heat differential between sand and metal. On February 5, F-111Fs attempted an experiment using their laser-guided bombs against enemy vehicles dispersed in the desert; these attacks were so successful that Horner, at Schwarzkopf's urgings, transferred the F-111Fs entirely into attacks in Kuwait. Dropping precision-guided bombs each night, the F-111Fs destroyed or damaged hundreds of Iraqi vehicles.

Aerial attacks significantly weakened the will to fight of Iraqi ground forces. Waves of B-52s pounded Iraqi positions, particularly the formidable Republican Guard units and the best Iraqi armored divisions. Meanwhile, psychological warfare efforts worked to weaken their morale further. Special radio programs broadcast antigovernment propaganda into Iraq, and aircraft dropped 30 million leaflets onto Iraqi positions. The constant bombardment severely demoralized the Iraqis, and a few deserters made their way across minefields into coalition hands in Kuwait. Larger numbers of deserters managed to flee into Turkey.

The Iraqis had entered Kuwait with a relatively well-equipped force manned by many combat-experienced soldiers and officers. At the end of the aerial operation, which lasted thirty-eight days and included more than 90,000 sorties, the coalition claimed to have destroyed 39 percent of the Iraqi tanks, 32 percent of the armored personnel carriers, and 48 percent of the artillery in Kuwait and southern Iraq. They also claimed to have destroyed more than one-third of the Iraqi aircraft, including thirty-five shot down in aerial combat. In addition to destroying much of the equipment and weakening the morale of the Iraqi army and air force, air strikes had destroyed key bridges across the Euphrates River, partially isolating the battlefield in preparation for the ground war. The final phase of the air attack, which gave priority to the support of ground operations, did not begin until after the launching of the ground attack.

The Hundred-Hour Ground Battle

Shortly before the ground assault, the Americans had about 527,000 troops in the Persian Gulf region, including those aboard ships. Among the U.S troops were seven U.S. Army divisions, three brigades from other divisions, two U.S. Marine divisions, and elements from a third marine division. Other large ground forces came from Great Britain, France, Egypt, and Syria, as well as Saudi Arabia and Kuwait. The coalition initially credited the Iraqis with having about 545,000 troops in southern Iraq and Kuwait, but by the time the ground assault began, the Iraqis may have had no more than 350,000 troops, including twelve armored divisions and thirty infantry divisions stationed in Kuwait and southern Iraq. Schwarzkopf later estimated that because of desertions and casualties, some Iraqi frontline divisions had less than 50 percent strength, and those in the second line had somewhere between 50–75 percent of their authorized strength.

To defend Kuwait, the Iraqis organized their defenses into three zones, similar to what they had done in the Iran-Iraq War. The first zone consisted of fortified defenses along the Saudi border and included two lines of infantry in bunkers and trenches behind huge sand berms, ditches filled with flammable oil, row after row of concertina wire, and minefields. The Iraqis expected these defenses to entangle the attacking coalition forces and expose them to massive artillery barrages, including chemicals. If the coalition's forces managed to penetrate this zone, they would then encounter the second defensive zone, which consisted of three Iraqi armored divisions poised to blunt any penetration. To the rear of these divisions, Republican Guard divisions occupied positions in a huge crescent pattern in southern Iraq. The Republican Guards functioned as a theater reserve, prepared to strike the coalition's forces with a massive counterattack if they managed to push through the forward two zones. Expecting an amphibious assault, the Iraqis also placed infantry divisions in strong defensive positions along the shores of the Persian Gulf. For reasons only Saddam understands, the western flank of the Iraqi forces had almost no defenses, providing the coalition an opening for a decisive blow.

To keep the Iraqis focused on the east, Schwarzkopf concocted an elaborate deception plan that convinced the Iraqis that the coalition's main attack would hit their main defenses in eastern Kuwait and that an amphibious assault near Kuwait City would also occur. Coalition forces remained in positions along the Kuwaiti border and conducted artillery raids and probes to create the impression that their attack would strike into the teeth of the Iraqi defenses in eastern Kuwait. At the same time, U.S. naval forces practiced for an amphibious landing along the Kuwaiti shoreline. These efforts convinced the Iraqis that major ground and amphibious assaults would advance directly into Iraq's strongest defenses and led them to hold six divisions in place along the coast of Kuwait.

Some observers described Schwarzkopf's campaign strategy as a "one-two punch" consisting of a "right jab" followed by a knockout blow from a "left hook." In the simplest terms, he concentrated his strength against the Iraqis' weakest point. With the Iraqis focused toward the east, Schwarzkopf intended to move west, sweep around front-line fortifications in Kuwait, and drive deep into Iraq in a gigantic envelopment. In preparation for the "left hook," Schwarzkopf began shifting forces far to the west of the Kuwaiti border with Iraq on January 17, three weeks prior to the launching of the ground attack. About 270,000 troops, complete with sixty days of ammunition and supplies, shifted west. The fact that the coalition had air supremacy made Schwarzkopf confident that the Iraqis would not detect this move, or if they did detect it, that they would not be able to shift most of their forces without exposing them to devastating air attacks.

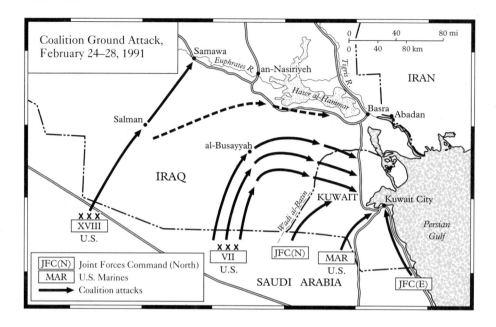

The Attack Begins

The ground attack was scheduled to begin on G-day, which was initially set for February 21, but a Russian peace initiative pushed G-day back. The coalition's ground attack officially began at 0400 hours on February 24. As part of the "right jab," Joint Forces Command East, consisting of five Saudi, Kuwaiti, Omani, and United Arab Emirate brigades, advanced between the coast and the main road leading to Kuwait City. To their left were the 1st and 2nd U.S. Marine divisions, reinforced by a U.S. Army armored brigade. The Joint Forces Command North, consisting of a combined Egyptian-Syrian force, advanced to the left of the marines but began moving later than the other forces to avoid having the Syrians' Soviet tanks accidentally engaged by the coalition's other forces.

As marines and other coalition forces advanced into eastern Kuwait, they passed through paths cleared through minefields and initially met only sporadic and uneven resistance. Nevertheless, two Iraqi mechanized brigades launched a counterattack and managed to come within 300 meters of the command post of 1st Marine Division. In the advance into Kuwait, the marines captured thousands of prisoners, as did other coalition forces. The numbers were so large that they slowed the advance of the attacking units.

As for the "left hook," VII Corps had the mission of advancing about one hundred kilometers into Iraq and then turning east into the rear and flank of the Iraqis. XVIII Airborne Corps was on VII Corps' left and had the mission of protecting the flank of the coalition's forces as they moved into Iraq. XVIII Airborne Corps was supposed to begin its move on G-day and VII Corps on G+1.

From an initial position about 300 kilometers west of the Kuwaiti border, XVIII Airborne Corps raced north toward the Euphrates River when the ground attack began on G-day, February 24. The corps consisted of 101st Airborne Division (Air Assault), 24th Infantry Division (Mechanized), a brigade of the 82nd Airborne Division, 3rd Armored Cavalry Regiment, and the French 6th Light Armored Division. In the largest air assault operation since Operation "Junction City" in the Vietnam War, 101st Airborne Division flew about 275 kilometers through driving rain to cut off the main highway between Baghdad and Kuwait. As the 101st moved forward rapidly, the French 6th Light Armored Division and a brigade from 82nd Airborne Division established a screen farther west to cover the flank and rear of the corps. Once the screen was established, 24th Infantry Division, with 3rd Armored Cavalry Regiment on its right, raced across the desert to link up with the 101st and block a crossing site over the Euphrates River just west of an-Nasiriyah. As soon as the Americans reached the Euphrates, Iraqi units could no longer move along the highway south of the Euphrates. Because of the water barrier formed by the Euphrates, the Hawr al-Hammar Lake, and extensive swamps, the Iraqis could escape only by crossing over hastily erected pontoon bridges across the Euphrates or withdrawing to the northeast toward Basra.

VII Corps had responsibility for delivering the knockout blow to the Republican Guard. Though the plan called for VII Corps to begin moving on G+1, the rapid advance of XVIII Corps and light opposition encountered by the "right jab" led Schwarzkopf to order VII Corps to begin moving on G-day. VII Corps included 1st Armored, 3rd Armored, 1st Infantry (Mechanized), and the British 1st Armored divisions, as well as 2nd Armored Cavalry Regiment. The Corps was reinforced by a brigade from 3rd Infantry Division (Mechanized), four field artillery brigades, and an aviation brigade. It numbered more than 145,000 soldiers and had more than 48,000 vehicles and aircraft. The magnitude of the logistical effort can be seen in the corps' expecting to consume more than 5.6 million gallons of fuel, 3.3 million gallons of water, and 6,075 tons of ammunition each day. When VII Corps moved into Iraq, hundreds of trucks followed closely behind; they carried tons of fuel, ammunition, and water to keep the huge force moving.

Ground Combat

VII Corps' attack passed through Iraqi defenses along the border easily. As 1st Cavalry Division created a diversion to the right of VII Corps by advancing up the Wadi al-Batin corridor, 2nd Armored Cavalry Regiment breached the border defenses and protected the rest of VII Corps' units as they moved into Iraq. 1st Armored Division, after crossing the border, moved to the left of 2nd Cavalry, and the two units led VII Corps' advance.

As 1st Armored Division raced forward, its initial objective was the town of al-Busayyah, about 110 kilometers inside Iraq. The town was an Iraqi logistics center on a main supply route and served as the headquarters for an Iraqi division. 1st Armored moved in a "compressed division wedge" formation twenty kilometers wide and fifty kilometers deep. With its cavalry squadron screening to the front, the division had its 1st Brigade as an advanced guard, its 2nd Brigade on its left, its 3rd Brigade on its right, its artillery between the two flank brigades, and its support elements (totaling nearly 1,000 vehicles) following closely.

On February 25, the VII Corps commander, Lieutenant General Frederick M. Franks, Jr., began turning his units to the east and inserting 3rd Armored Division between 1st Armored Division and 2nd Cavalry Regiment. By the time 1st Armored Division began turning, it had already moved about 150 kilometers in forty-one hours. Using the analogy of a hand closing into a fist, General Franks sought to concentrate his divisions and to destroy the Republican Guard. He soon had four divisions on line, including the 1st Armored, 3rd Armored, 1st Infantry, and British 1st Armored, and pressed the attack against the Republic Guard units and the north-south Basra–Kuwait City highway.

Before General Franks concentrated his divisions into a fist, 2nd Armored Cavalry Regiment took part in some of the heaviest combat of the war. When the Iraqi 12th Armored and Republican Guards Tawakalna divisions, as well as other units, attempted to pull out of Kuwait, they ran directly into 2nd Armored Cavalry. Much of the fighting occurred in a blinding sandstorm on February 26 with sporadic concentrations of Iraqi artillery falling on the Americans' position. Though visibility in the sandstorm was sometimes less than 200 meters, the M1A1 tanks' thermal sights could see almost one kilometer, and the Americans extracted a terrible toll from the waves of tanks that came charging toward them. Despite desperate

Iraqi tank crews had little chance of success since they were out-gunned by American tanks and not prepared to fight large armored formations. Not one American M1A1 tank was lost to Iraqi tank fire.

charges and the sacrifice of many lives, the Iraqis never managed to break out of the deadly trap that had closed behind them.

Though pounded by coalition air forces for weeks, the Republican Guard managed to shift some units from a southeast to a southwest orientation and awaited the arrival of VII Corps. The Republican Guards sometimes occupied strong defensive positions, but the superiority of the M1A1 tank proved decisive. The M1A1 could fire at and hit armored vehicles three kilometers away, well beyond the effective range of the Iraqi T-72s. Aerial attacks increased the effect of the ground attack. While American ground forces engaged tanks and armored personnel carriers, coalition air forces destroyed numerous enemy vehicles as they attempted to maneuver or escape. By the end of the campaign, only 700 of Iraq's tanks survived.

As the final thrust of the "left hook" continued forward, elements from 24th Infantry Division and 3rd Armored Cavalry Regiment attempted to close up on VII Corps' left flank. As the coalition's forces moved forward on February 27, the fourth day of the attack, they met alternating pockets of Iraqi soldiers ready to fight or to surrender. Around 1800 hours on the 27th the cavalry squadron of 1st Infantry Division reached the Basra–Kuwait City highway; the bulk of the division was about ten kilometers to its rear. Throughout the night of February 27–28, elements in the corps wiped out pockets of resistance left in their rear until the "cessation of offensive operations," proposed by Washington and accepted by Schwarzkopf, occurred at 0800 hours on the 28th.

Assessing the Victory

Although elements of the "left hook" had moved a great distance (the 24th Division traveled about 370 kilometers) in an attempt to close the "trap" completely, a sizable number of Iraqi units escaped on the nights of February 26 and 27 by fleeing to the northeast toward Basra. This opened Schwarzkopf and Franks to criticism for having failed to close that escape route and for having failed to destroy even more of Iraq's forces. The magnitude of the coalition's victory after forty-two days, however, can be seen in the estimates of damage done to the Iraqis. About one month after the cease-fire, U.S. intelligence agencies estimated that 85 percent of the Iraqi tanks, 50 percent of the armored personnel carriers, and 90 percent of the artillery in southern Iraq or Kuwait were damaged or destroyed. More than 10,000 Iraqi prisoners were taken in the first twenty-four hours of the ground battle, and more than 70,000 by its end. Although no final figure could be obtained, the Defense Intelligence Agency (DIA) estimated several months after the end of the war that the Iraqis suffered 100,000 soldiers killed and 300,000 wounded, and that 150,000 Iraqis had deserted. Acknowledging the difficulty of making estimates of enemy casualties, the DIA stated that its estimate had an "error factor" of 50 percent or higher. In sharp contrast to the Iraqi losses, the coalition suffered few. A total of eighty-nine Americans died in the war, including thirty-eight in the four-day ground battle, and 324 were wounded, including seventy-eight in the ground battle.

Though exact Iraqi losses may never be known, the coalition had destroyed most of Saddam's armed forces and thereby significantly reduced his abili ty to threaten Kuwait. An advance on Baghdad, as some critics suggested, might have resulted in the overthrow of Saddam, but the coalition's goal had been to repel the Iraqi invaders from Kuwait, not to destroy Saddam's government.

Throughout the war, relations between the military and the news media were strained. Before the ground attack began, news reporters had only limited access to military personnel and were usually accompanied by escorts. In an attempt to fool the Iraqis into thinking that the coalition's main attack would hit the coast and would include an amphibious assault against Kuwait, however, Schwarzkopf permitted news reporters to broadcast live pictures of U.S. Marines conducting practice landings. Only after the ground battle began did news reporters gain greater access to other units participating in the operation. Another controversial aspect of war came from the broadcasting of reports from Baghdad. News reporters from the West provided live pictures of the aerial attack on Iraq and on bomb damage. Critics accused them of being used by the Iraqis to influence public opinion in the West; this led one news reporter to respond, "We're using them, they're using us." In the final analysis, the ability to transmit live television coverage from throughout the battle area intensified the desire of the military to control the access of reporters, while simultaneously increasing the desire of the news media for greater access.

In retrospect, Schwarzkopf's campaign strategy and the superiority of his forces were the keys to his victory. Weakened by thirty-eight days of air attack and surprised by the swiftness and the depth of the American move, the Iraqis simply could not respond adequately to the coalition's "left hook." The relentless aerial attack had severely weakened the Iraqi forces, and the ground attack defeated them completely. Though some of the Iraqi forces escaped, Saddam had foolishly placed his forces in a vulnerable position, had played to the strength of the coalition, particularly the Americans, and had offered a challenge the international community could not ignore.

The United Nations: From Peacekeeping to Peace Enforcement

During the Cold War, the United Nations often conducted peace-keeping operations where some semblance of peace existed and where the former combatants asked for U.N. assistance. Following the sending of officers into the Balkans and Indonesia in 1947, the U.N. began its first official peace-keeping operation in May 1948 with the establishment of the United Nations Truce Supervision Organization. U.N. forces subsequently participated in more than twenty-five peace-keeping missions in such diverse areas as Lebanon, the Congo, Yemen, Cyprus, the Dominican Republic, India-Pakistan, Angola, El Salvador, and Cambodia. Over half a million people served in U.N. peace-keeping forces after 1948, of which more than 800 from forty-three countries lost their lives. Always invited by both sides and always attempting to show impartiality, the U.N. forces sought to maintain peace by establishing a cease-fire between belligerents, serving as buffers between opposing forces, overseeing the implementation of peace plans, and providing humanitarian relief. Other missions included disarming guerrillas, preserving law and order, and monitoring elections.

After the Cold War ended in 1989–1990, the number of U.N. peace-keeping operations increased from an average of three or four in a year (several lasting for decades) to thirteen in December 1992. As the number of operations increased, and as violence and turmoil expanded in the aftermath of the Cold War, the United Nations asserted its right to intervene—without invitation—in the internal affairs of sovereign states. The U.N. Secretary General, Boutros Boutros-Ghali, emphasized the principle of "universal sovereignty" and the "legitimate involvement" of the United Nations "in issues affecting the world as a whole." Using the term "peace enforcement" to describe a military intervention by the United Nations, he called for multinational operations to end hostilities and enable diplomats to negotiate a final peace. He defined such diplomatic efforts as "peacemaking."

One of the first post–Cold War international interventions occurred at the end of the Persian Gulf War, when the Kurds in northern Iraq revolted against the authority of Saddam Hussein. The United Nations authorized humanitarian relief to the Kurds and forbade the Iraqis to interfere with relief efforts. The United States and other member nations soon conducted relief operations in Operation "Provide Comfort." A year later in Operation "Southern Watch," American and other nations' aircraft prevented the Iraqis from using air power against Shi'ites in southern Iraq. In essence, the U.N. enforced the peace over the objections of Saddam's government and went beyond providing observers for a cease-fire.

Somalia

Another crisis involving intervention by the U.N. occurred in Somalia. Despite the optimism of the international community, the complexities and difficulties of intervening with multinational forces quickly became apparent. The roots of the crisis came from prolonged drought, overpopulation, and decades of war—clan, ethnic, and religious—which turned Somalia into a scene of terrible human suffering. Although most Somalis speak the same language and are Sunni Muslims, the area has a long history of conflict between clan and tribal groups. Violence increased through the 1980s when the powers of the central government waned. As banditry and fighting between clans disrupted commerce and agriculture, many Somalis fled from their rural homes to cities or towns where they found some safety but little or no food. The situation worsened in 1991 when the central government

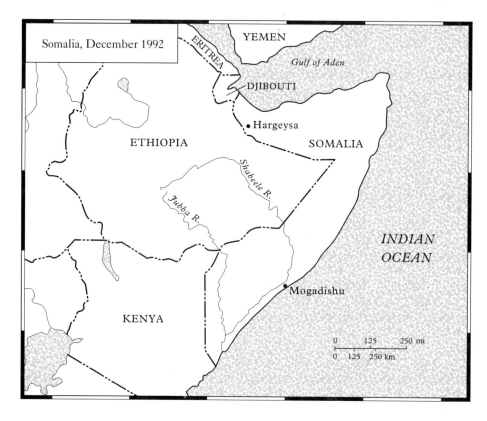

Somalia, December 1992

collapsed. By October 1992, hundreds of Somalis were dying daily from starvation. To alleviate the suffering, international relief agencies attempted to transport food to the starving Somalis, but bandits and clan members looted most of the supplies. A small U.N. force provided some security but had little effect. The United States dispatched large amounts of food to Somalia and saved numerous lives, but the violence and banditry continued.

As the situation in Somalia became more desperate and famine worsened, the United Nations decided to intervene. Though it had long refused to intervene in a sovereign country without an invitation, the U.N. Security Council decided that the magnitude of the "human tragedy" in Somalia had become a "threat to international peace and security" and thereby a legitimate object of U.N. action. Following the approval of a U.N. Security Council Resolution, President George Bush announced to the American people on December 4, 1992, that as part of the United Nations' effort he had ordered a "substantial force" to Somalia. The U.S. forces had the mission of creating "a secure environment in the hardest-hit parts of Somalia" and then passing the security mission to a U.N. peace-keeping force and withdrawing. Other states agreeing to send forces were France, Pakistan, Morocco, Malaysia, Italy, Belgium, Canada, Australia, and Egypt, but the largest number came from the United States.

As part of Operation "Restore Hope," the first Americans, U.S. Marines, landed at Mogadishu before dawn on December 9. The plan called for about 16,000 marines and 10,000 soldiers to land in Somalia. Americans established some control over Mogadishu and in subsequent days fanned out across the southern half of Somalia. By the end of December, the U.S. had 12,500 troops in Somalia, and seventeen other countries had 6,000. Planners envisaged a U.N. force of about 28,000 peacekeepers (3,000–5,000 Americans) eventually taking over the operation. In the middle of January 1993, the first Americans departed as military personnel from other countries began replacing them. By May most of the American personnel came from the U.S. Army's 10th Mountain Division.

Throughout this period, U.S. leaders resisted expanding their mission from providing humanitarian aid to disarming feuding clans. U.N. officials believed that if the Somalis were not disarmed, clashes between the clans would occur and starvation would return when international forces departed. Despite reservations about expanding their mission, American forces began seizing weapons, particularly in Mogadishu, after several incidents, but their focus remained on providing humanitarian aid.

In early May, the United Nations took control of the multinational effort, and Lieutenant General Cevik Bir of Turkey became its commander. Almost simultaneously, efforts to disarm the Somalis escalated, and low-level urban guerrilla warfare began. U.N. casualties also rose rapidly. In June, fighting erupted in and around Mogadishu between U.N. peace-keeping forces and Somalis loyal to General Mohammed Farah Aidid, one of the region's most powerful warlords. As U.N. forces operated in the Mogadishu area, they received sniper fire and became engaged in firefights. While returning on June 5 from an inspection, a Pakistani unit was caught in a three-sided ambush. By the end of the day, twenty-three Pakistani soldiers had died, and sixty-three other U.N. soldiers had been wounded.

The following day, the U.N. Security Council condemned the attacks and called for the "arrest and detention" of those responsible. In subsequent weeks, U.N. troops attempted to capture Aidid and had several skirmishes with his forces. Differences emerged among the coalition with the Italians' being particularly critical of the abandonment of neutrality and the shift away from humanitarian efforts. In mid-July, U.N. officials relieved the commander of the Italian contingent in the multinational force after he refused to engage his 2,500 troops in action against Aidid.

In late August, soldiers from the U.S. Army's Delta Force and 75th Ranger Regiment arrived and launched raids in search of Aidid and his top aides. On October 3, however, they suffered heavy losses in Mogadishu when a "snatch operation" went badly wrong. The raid went well at first, for the Americans captured several of Aidid's aides. But as they withdrew, the Somalis, using a rocket-propelled grenade, shot down a helicopter from 160th Special Operations Regiment. When the Americans moved to secure the helicopter, the Somalis shot down another helicopter. Then several hundred fighters loyal to Aidid rushed to the area and began pouring fire into the surrounded Americans. A rapid reaction force consisting of a company from the 10th Mountain Division attempted to rescue the surrounded rangers, but Somalis ambushed the truck-borne troops as they moved through the city's narrow streets. A relief column of American infantry, four Pakistani tanks, and Malaysian armored personnel carriers finally reached the Americans, but by the time the fighting stopped, eighteen American and one Malaysian peacekeeper had died and more than one hundred were wounded. During the battle, the Somalis may have captured and executed several Americans; they kept one pilot as a prisoner but finally released him. Estimates of the number of Somalis killed in the fighting on October 3 ranged from 200 to 300, including women and children.

Shortly after the battle, President Bill Clinton spelled out a more limited mission for American forces. This included keeping key roads and lines of communication open for relief workers and food supplies, maintaining pressure on those who had originally cut off the flow of relief supplies, and helping the Somali people "solve their own problems." In essence, the Americans had halted their efforts to capture Aidid and disarm the factions. Clinton also announced that American forces would withdraw prior to March 31, 1994. Other states eventually joined the exodus from Somalia. Despite the magnitude of the continuing human tragedy, members of the United Nations no longer perceived Somalia as a "threat to international peace and security."

Bosnia-Herzegovina

The United Nations also experienced difficulties in Yugoslavia where it found itself torn between—on the one hand—providing humanitarian relief and local security or—on the other hand—intervening and using force to halt a wave of slaughter, rape, and destruction. The crisis began in February 1991 when the northern republics of Slovenia and Croatia adopted measures that pushed them toward independence from Yugoslavia. After Slovenia and Croatia formally declared their independence in June, Yugoslavian federal troops intervened to halt the breakup of their state, but on December 19, Germany recognized the two breakaway republics. Two weeks later, after the United Nations promised to deploy peace-keeping forces in Croatia, the Yugoslav government accepted the breakup and agreed to a peace plan and a cease-fire.

The disintegration of Yugoslavia accelerated in early 1992 when citizens of the republic of Bosnia-Herzegovina held a referendum and overwhelmingly supported independence. With a population of about 4.4 million, 44 percent of the Bosnians were Muslim Slavs, 31 percent Serbs, and 17 percent Croats. Most of the Serbs belonged to the Eastern Orthodox Church, and most of the Croats to the Roman Catholic Church. Large-scale violence began in early April when Serbian militia and guerrillas seized control of much of Bosnia. In May, the president of Serbia (previously Yugoslavia) transferred substantial arms and ammunition and about 50,000 Yugoslav troops to the control of Bosnian Serbs. Widespread atrocities occurred as the Serbs tightened their control over most of Bosnia, occupied about 70 percent of the countryside, and forced about one million Muslims and Croats to become refugees. The fighting quickly degenerated into a three-sided civil war.

In May the United Nations imposed economic sanctions on Yugoslavia and established an embargo against the shipment of weapons to

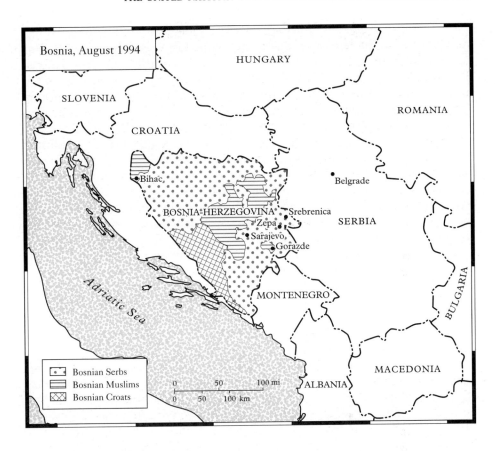

Bosnia, but it stopped short of using force. While the Serbs received weapons from the Yugoslavian army and the Croats from Croatia, the Muslims had few weapons, and the U.N. embargo hampered their acquiring additional weapons. As the carnage continued, the United Nations issued an ultimatum in late June for the Serbs to stop shelling Sarajevo. When the bombardment slowed, the United Nations began airlifting food and medicine to Sarajevo. Meanwhile, Serbs continued terrorizing other Bosnian towns. The United Nations responded by banning military flights over Bosnia but initially did little to enforce the ban.

As the crisis intensified, evidence mounted of Serbian atrocities against civilians. Bosnian refugees reported that Serbian forces had massacred Muslims and Croats and established concentration camps in which they tortured and killed thousands. At the end of December the Bosnian government estimated that 150,000 Bosnians had been killed and 1.6 million made homeless. In early January 1993, a team of European Community investigators reported that approximately 20,000 Muslim women had been raped by Serbian soldiers. Many of the victims claimed that the Serbs had used rape as a "weapon of war." The investigators concluded that thousands of rapes had served the "strategic purpose" of "ethnic cleansing" by "demoralizing and terrorizing communities" and driving the Bosnians from their homes.

Despite evidence of slaughter, mass rapes, and "ethnic cleansing," the United Nations refused to use force or risk losing its neutrality. Believing the Bosnian problem could best be handled through negotiations, Boutros-Ghali insisted that U.N. military intervention could only make the situation worse and could draw the international organization into a long and costly war. Nonetheless, he placed U.N. forces in Bosnia but restricted their role; he made them responsible primarily for escorting relief supplies into Sarajevo and other besieged areas. Once on the ground, U.N. military commanders argued against the aerial bombing of Serbian positions around Sarajevo because of their fears of retaliation against U.N. ground forces. In late February 1993, with U.N. approval, U.S. Air Force planes began parachuting food and medical supplies to Muslim towns besieged by the Serbs. In March, French and German planes also began dropping relief supplies and in April, NATO aircraft began enforcing a "no-fly zone" over Bosnia's airspace. Beginning in June, talks in Geneva between the warring Serbian, Croatian, and Muslim factions of Bosnia-Herzegovina focused on dividing Bosnia into three ethnic states. With the talks yielding little, the U.N. Security Council declared Sarajevo and five other Muslim strongholds in Bosnia "safe areas" and agreed to send U.N. troops to guard them. Nevertheless, Serbian and Croatian forces prevented U.N. ground forces from entering Muslim enclaves, and the wanton killing continued.

As the horror of the international community increased, the U.N. began using limited force against the Serbs. After a mortar round killed 68 civilians in a public market in Sarajevo in February 1994, the United Nations, threatening air strikes, ordered the Serbs to withdraw heavy weapons from around Sarajevo or hand them over to U.N. forces; the Serbs reluctantly complied. In late February, NATO observers identified six Serbian planes blatantly violating the U.N. ban on flights over Bosnian airspace, and two American planes shot four of them down. Technically, it was the first combat operation by NATO forces. In April, with U.N. authorization, NATO planes bombed Serbian forces around Gorazde, a safe area, after they refused U.N. demands to stop shelling and withdraw. After some delays and negotiations, the Serbs finally agreed to withdraw their heavy weapons beyond twenty kilometers from Gorazde; nearly 400 U.N. troops deployed to monitor the Serbian withdrawal. In August and September, NATO planes hit Serbian heavy weapons when they entered a zone around Sarajevo from which heavy weapons had been excluded.

The conflict took an unexpected turn in November after Muslim forces attacked out of the safe area around Bihac and drove the Serbs back. The Serbs counterattacked and soon placed great pressure—including aerial attacks—on Bihac. In late November, NATO planes launched limited strikes against a Serbian-controlled airbase in Croatia, hitting the airfield and avoiding planes and fuel dumps; they also struck Serb missile sites on the outskirts of Bihac. The Serbs, however, continued attacking Bihac and detained more than 450 U.N. personnel as hostages. Air strikes against the Serbs quickly ended. The American secretary of defense, William J. Perry, stated publicly that Serbian gains could not be reversed, and some Western political leaders called for new peace proposals acceptable to the Serbs. In

Many of the combatants in the Balkans had little or no military training and had no reservations about destroying civilian lives and property and committing atrocities.

May 1995 the Serbs began bombarding Bosnian safe areas and forcibly taking back the heavy weapons they had previously yielded to U.N. custody. When the United Nations responded with NATO air strikes, the Serbs again seized U.N. troops as hostages and human shields. As the crisis worsened, the Serbs shot down a U.S. Air Force F-16 fighter.

Fifteen NATO and European defense ministers met to discuss the crisis and decided to increase the combat strength of U.N. forces in Bosnia by sending two rapid reaction brigades to Bosnia. While the British 24th Airmobile Brigade could respond rapidly to an attack on U.N. troops in a remote area, Task Force Alpha (a brigade consisting of French, British, and Dutch troops and light armored vehicles) could provide rapid reinforcement and armored protection. Some critics believed that by adding the two brigades U.N. forces risked crossing the "Mogadishu line" and forfeiting their neutrality. European leaders, however, insisted that the U.N. troops would remain peacekeepers and not become combatants.

Despite the United Nations' reluctance to use force, its role gradually had expanded from humanitarian relief to peace enforcement. It simultaneously had tried to use carefully calibrated air attacks to compel the Serbs to comply with its ultimatums and small ground forces to provide humanitarian aid and local security, particularly around the so-called safe areas. The unwillingness of U.N. members to be drawn into a wider war and the vulnerability of peace-keeping forces on the ground, however, restricted the peace enforcement efforts of the United Nations. The limited power of international forces became even more apparent in July when the Serbs captured the safe area at Srebrenica and expelled thousands of terrified Muslim refugess.

In both Bosnia and Somalia, military officials criticized the ad hoc nature and inefficiency of U.N. military operations. In their eyes, the conflicting interests and objectives of participating states made it difficult to identify clear missions for multinational military forces and precise conditions for their withdrawal. Moreover, the diversity of forces involved in U.N. operations made detailed coordination difficult; and a weak and diffuse chain of command, unreliable intelligence, incompatible communications equipment, and the absence of a common logistical system added further complexities. Not until operations were fully under way in Somalia and Bosnia, for example, did the U.N. establish a twenty-four-hour operations center in its headquarters. To some, deficiencies in the U.N. system ruled out swift, decisive interventions unless one or two states dominated the entire operation. Some analysts called for the establishment of a standing U.N. "rapid deployment force" or "peace-enforcement unit" which could deter or repel aggression by being transported to distant regions on short notice. Member states, however, remained opposed to a standing U.N. army. Despite the apparent limitations of multinational forces, U.N. Secretary General Boutros-Ghali remained convinced of their utility and did not abandon his call for international peace-enforcement operations with personnel from as many as "forty states."

*   *   *   *

Throughout the post–World War II period, major military powers often sent expeditions to distant regions to conduct combat operations. Relying on air and sea transport, most expeditions deployed rapidly on short notice to unfamiliar locations such as the Dominican Republic, the Falkland Islands, or Grenada. The expeditions usually sought to overwhelm a poorly armed or less capable opponent quickly. Despite the relative brevity of the campaigns, the expeditions faced complex challenges; intervening forces frequently had to transport troops and equipment hastily over long distances and rely on combinations of air, sea, and land forces to gain victory swiftly. Since the operations typically took place in unexpected and unfamiliar locations, the intervening forces often encountered significant difficulties in obtaining adequate intelligence, securing sufficient logistical support, establishing effective communications, and accomplishing proper coordination. Advances in strategic transport and communications, nevertheless, provided a few states a true "global reach." As the Cold War faded from the scene, interventions by national or multinational forces in regional conflicts appeared likely in a world plagued by national, religious, ethnic, and regional antagonisms.

Iraq's aggression against Kuwait, however, provoked the first major conflict of the post–Cold War era, the Persian Gulf War. Those opposing the Iraqis brought with them forces and methods designed for high-intensity conflict in central Europe, and in the subsequent fighting, they provided an impressive display of advanced methods and weapons. After witnessing the swift defeat of Iraq and the remarkable performance of the coalition's forces in the Persian Gulf War, some analysts suggested that weapons based on the electronic microchip would replace the low-cost, mass-production weapons of the industrial age that had dominated warfare through much of the nineteenth and twentieth centuries. Highly lethal and accurate weapons would supposedly enable leaders to wage intense battles of short duration, rather than grinding battles of attrition. Increases in tactical, operational, and strategic mobility also suggested new possibilities for using maneuver against an opponent. Other advances in intelligence-gathering systems and in communications systems suggested new means of commanding and controlling military units, and the wide use of computers facilitated the processing of massive amounts of information. Those believing a new age of warfare had begun saw the need for new strategies, new tactics, and new relationships between military organizations and societies.

Despite such expectations, the initial challenges of the new post–Cold War era found little use for new strategies and tactics and only limited use for high-technology weapons. Amidst the spread of violence and turmoil, armed forces found themselves acting as peacekeepers and having to deal not with disciplined, well-equipped opponents but with paramilitary forces, militias, and gangster-like elements. In this environment, the United Nations expanded its role from peacekeeping to peace enforcement. In Bosnia the United Nations initially provided relief supplies to people besieged by forces attempting to starve them into submission, but the U.N. secretary general gradually permitted U.N. forces to use limited force. In Somalia, the United Nations intervened without a formal invitation, and the role of the intervening forces also expanded from providing humanitarian aid to peace enforcement. The reluctance of the United Nations to act more forcefully in Bosnia and Somalia and the difficulties encountered in both areas, however, demonstrated the complexities of interventions—whether launched by a single state or by a multinational force.

SUGGESTED READINGS

Adkin, Mark. *Urgent Fury: The Battle for Grenada* (Lexington, Mass.: D.C. Heath, 1989).

Atkinson, Rick. *Crusade: The Untold Story of the Persian Gulf War* (Boston: Houghton Mifflin, 1993).

Blechman, Barry M., and Stephen S. Kaplain. *Force Without War: U.S. Armed Forces as a Political Instrument* (Washington, D.C.: The Brookings Institute, 1978).

Bolger, Daniel P. *Americans at War: 1975–1986, An Era of Violent Peace* (Novato, Calif.: Presidio Press, 1988).

Callwell, C. E. *Small Wars: Their Principles and Practice* (London: Her Majesty's Stationery Office, 1899).

Dunn, Peter M., and Bruce W. Watson, eds. *American Intervention in Grenada: The Implications of Operation "Urgent Fury"* (Boulder, Col.: Westview Press, 1985).

Friedman, Norman. *Desert Victory: The War for Kuwait* (Annapolis: Naval Institute Press, 1991).

Hallion, Richard P. *Storm over Iraq: Air Power and the Gulf War* (Washington, D.C.: Smithsonian Institution Press, 1992).

Hastings, Max, and Simon Jenkins. *The Battle for the Falklands* (New York: W. W. Norton and Company, 1983).

Koburger, Charles W., Jr. *Sea Power in the Falklands* (New York: Praeger, 1983).

Middlebrook, Martin. *The Fight for the "Malvinas": The Argentine Forces in the Falklands War* (New York: Viking, 1989).

Musicant, Ivan. *The Banana Wars: A History of United States Military Intervention in Latin America from the Spanish–American War to the Invasion of Panama* (New York: Macmillan, 1990).

Odom, Thomas P. *Dragon Operations: Hostage Rescues in the Congo, 1964–1965* (Fort Leavenworth, Kans.: Combat Studies Institute, 1988).

Scales, Robert H., Jr. *Certain Victory: United States Army in the Gulf War* (Washington, D.C.: Government Printing Office, 1993).

Shaughnessy, Hugh. *Grenada: An Eyewitness Account of the U.S. Invasion and the Caribbean History that Provoked It* (New York: Dodd, Mead and Company, 1984).

Spector, Ronald H. *U.S. Marines in Grenada, 1983* (Washington, D.C.: Government Printing Office, 1987).

Spiller, Roger J. *"Not War But Like War": The American Intervention in Lebanon* (Fort Leavenworth, Kans.: Combat Studies Institute, 1981).

Summers, Harry G., Jr. *On Strategy II: A Critical Appraisal of the Gulf War* (New York: Dell Publishing, 1992).

United Nations. *The Blue Helmets: A Review of United Nations Peace-keeping* (New York: United Nations Department of Public Information, 1990).

Watson, Bruce W., and Peter G. Tsouras, eds. *Operation Just Cause: The U.S. Intervention in Panama* (Boulder, Col.: Westview Press, 1991).

Yates, Lawrence A. *Power Pack: U.S. Intervention in the Dominican Republic, 1964–1966* (Fort Leavenworth, Kans.: Combat Studies Institute, 1988).

PHOTOGRAPH CREDITS

Chapter 1: p. 3, Los Alamos National Laboratories; p. 9, National Archives; p. 12, National Archives; p. 17, The Bettmann Archive; p. 21, National Archives; p. 25, National Archives. **Chapter 2:** p. 32, National Archives; p. 41, Wide World; p. 42, National Archives; p. 45, National Archives; p. 52, Wide World; p. 53, UPI/Bettmann. **Chapter 3:** p. 60, Wide World; p. 65, UPI/Bettmann; p. 71, UPI/Bettmann; p. 75, UPI/Bettmann; p. 77, Frank Wolfe/LBJ Library Collection; p. 86, UPI/Bettmann. **Chapter 4:** p. 98, UPI/Bettmann; p. 108, Wide World; p. 113, Gamma Liaison. **Chapter 5:** p. 126, UPI/Bettmann; p. 129, UPI/Bettmann; p. 131, © 1995 Abbas/Magnum Photos, Inc.; p. 137, Wide World; p. 142, Courtesy of Raytheon; p. 148, Wide World; p. 157, Reuters/Bettmann.

Index

The Absolute Weapon (Brodie), 14
Abu Ageila, 94; battle of (June 1967), 97
"Admirals' Revolt," 5
Afghanistan, Soviet war in (1979–1988), 23, 110–117, 111 map
Aidid, General Mohammed Farah, 153
Airborne forces: British, 128; Iraqi, 109; Israeli, 94, 97; U.S., 133–134
Airborne operations: Falklands, 128; in Iran-Iraq War, 109; Operation "Urgent Fury," 133–134; in Sinai campaign (1956), 94
Air cavalry (U.S.), 72
Aircraft. See Helicopters
Aircraft types, British design, Sea Harrier (VSTOL fighter), 126
Aircraft types, French design: Mirage (fighter), 126; Super Etendard (fighter-bomber), 126
Aircraft types, Soviet design: MiG-15 (fighter), 49; Tu-16 Badger (bomber), 12; Tu-20 Bear (bomber), 12
Aircraft types, U.S. design: A-7 Skyhawk (fighter-bomber), 126, 134; B-26 (bomber), 49; B-29 Superfortress (bomber), 5; B-36 (bomber), 5–6; B-47 Stratojet (bomber), 11–12, 18; B-52 Stratofortress (bomber), 11–12, 70, 74–75, 82, 86–87, 141; B-54, 144; C-5 Galaxy (transport), 123; C-47 Dakota (transport), 71; C-119 Flying Boxcar (transport), 123; C-130 Hercules (transport), 123, 133; C-141B Starlifter (transport), 123; EA-6B Prowler (electronic warfare), 141; F-4G Wild Weasel (electronic warfare), 141; F-5 Freedom Fighter (fighter-bomber), 75 illus.; F-15E (fighter-bomber), 141; F-16 (fighter), 157; F-105 Thunderchief (fighter-bomber), 70; F-111F (fighter-bomber), 142, 144; F-117A (stealth attack), 139, 141–143; F/A-18 Hornet (fighter-bomber), 141; U-2 (reconnaissance), 12, 18–19

Aircraft types, Vertical/Short Take-off and Landing (VSTOL), 124; British Sea Harrier (VSTOL fighter), 126
Air defense. See Missiles, air defense
Air Force, Israeli, 97
Air Force, Soviet. See Aircraft types, Soviet design
Air Force, U.S.: aerial interceptor squadrons, 13; airlifts to Bosnia-Herzegovina, 156; in Korean War, 36–37, 53; in nuclear warfare, 11–13, 22–24; in Persian Gulf War, 138–144; in Vietnam War, 70. See also Aircraft types, U.S. design
Air forces, United Nations, in Korean War, 33, 49. See also Air Force, U.S.
Airlift: Berlin Blockade, 5; Bosnia-Herzegovina, 155–156
Air power. See Air Force, U.S.; Korean War; Persian Gulf War; Vietnam War
Albany (Landing Zone), 74
Almond, Major General Edward M., 37
Ambush tactics, 64, 67, 80, 153; in Afghanistan, 23, 110–117, 111 map
Amphibious operations: Falklands, 127–128; Iran-Iraq War, 109; Korean War, 36–37, 39; Operation "Urgent Fury," 132; Persian Gulf War, 145
Angola, 116
An Loc, 87
Antisubmarine warfare, 13
Antiwar demonstrations (Vietnam War), 84
Ap Bac, battle of (January 1963), 67–68
Aqaba, Gulf of, 95–96
Arab-Israeli wars, 93–104, 117. See also Casualties, Arab-Israeli wars
Arab League, 136
"Arab solution" to Persian Gulf War, 136
Argentina, 108 illus., 124–130, 125 map, 126 illus., 129 illus.
Arizona Line, 44, 44 map
Armed forces, United Nations, 35, 39